The Guide to Translation and Localization

Communicating in the Global Marketplace

8th Edition

by

Copyright © 2018 by LanguageLine Translation Solutions

Copyright and Reprint Permissions: Abstracting is permitted with credit to the source. Libraries are permitted to photocopy isolated pages beyond the limits of US copyright law for private use of their patrons. For other copying, reprint, or publication permission write to LanguageLine Translation Solutions, 15115 SW Sequoia Parkway, Suite 100, Portland, Oregon 97224.

Library of Congress Number 2017963467
ISBN 9780998625508

Additional copies can be ordered from:

LanguageLine Translation Solutions
15115 SW Sequoia Parkway
Suite 100
Portland, OR 97224
Tel: 503-419-4856
Toll Free: 1-800-878-8523
FAX: 503-419-4873

www.languageline.com/translation-localization
info@LLTS.com

Eighth edition printed in the United States of America

Editor: Scott Ludwigsen
Managing Editor: Zac Westbrook
Copy Editor: Jennifer Polis
Art Director: Pete Landers
Design: Pete Landers

Contributing Writers: Many thanks to all of our employees past and present who have contributed to this and previous editions of *The Guide to Translation and Localization*.

All brand or product names, trademarks, service marks, and copyrights are the property of their respective owners.

cover photo by rawpixel.com

Table of Contents

Welcome Letter from the CEO 1

President's Message 3

Introduction - Making the Case for Translation

Building a Business Case for Language Services 5

Section 1 - Behind the Curtain (The Science of Languages Services)

1 - What Are Language Services 9

2 - I'm Ready. How Do I Get it Done? 13

3 - Don't Just Google It 16

4 - Planning a Successful Project 19

5 - Quality: Every Buyer Wants It and Every Vendor Sells It,
    but What is It? 25

6 - Process is the Key to Success 31

7 - Preparing Your Content for Localization 38

8 - DTP: The Shapes of Language 42

9 - How Do You Know If It's Any Good? 48

10 - Getting the Language Right 55

Section 2 - Building Solutions

11 - It's the Law: Complying with Language Access Mandates
     at the State and Local Government Level 62

12 - Take It to the Bank, Banco or 银行: Translation for
     Financial Institutions 69

13 - Side Effects May Include Higher Patient Satisfaction, Reduced Costs, and Better Health
     Outcomes - Language Access for Health Care Organizations 73

Section 3 - Sexy Stuff for Gearheads

14 - Localization Engineering 77

15 - Translation Memory and Terminology Management 83

16 - Translation Management Systems, Connectors,
     and Automation 88

17 - Localizing Web Content With a Translation Proxy 93

18 - Content Management Systems 97

19 - Machine Translation 103

Section 4 - On Demand Interpretation

20 - Over-the-Phone Interpretation 108

21 - Video Remote Interpretation 114

22 - Onsite Interpretation 119

23 - Language Proficiency Testing 123

Section 5 - Keeping the Pulse of the Industry

24 - Straight to the Source with Clarity[SM] 126

25 - Builders, Breakers and Defenders 129

Contributors 133

Welcome Letter
From the CEO

Scott Klein, CEO

Scott is a seasoned executive with many years of leadership experience and success with achieving profitable growth in a variety of industries. Most recently Scott held the position of CEO of SuperMedia, Inc., a print and online publisher of yellow pages. Prior to that, Scott served as President and CEO of Information Resources, Inc. (IRI), a leading market research firm; President of the Consumer Industries, Retail & Energy division of Electronic Data Systems Corporation (EDS); President of PCMall, Inc., a $1.2 billion telesales, catalogue and Internet reseller of computer-related products; Executive VP and COO for PrimeSource Building Products; as well as leadership roles with Pepsico Inc.; and Procter & Gamble Company.

A graduate of Syracuse University, Scott holds a bachelor's degree in accounting.

Regardless of industry, there has never been a greater need for translation and localization.

The numbers are staggering: According to the Census Bureau, 20 percent of US residents speak a language other than English at home, while 8 percent are limited English proficient, meaning they speak English less than "very well." The latter figure has grown 80 percent since 1990, from 14 million to the current 25 million.

In all, an incredible 350 languages are spoken in households across America.

As remarkable as these figures seem today, they are expected to grow even more in the near future. Multiculturals accounted for 92 percent of the total growth of the nation's population between 2000 and 2015, and now make up 38 percent of the US population. According to Nielsen data, this group is projected to increase by 2.3 million each year before becoming a majority of the population by 2044.

At the same time, more products are being shipped around the globe and more services are being delivered worldwide than ever before. Stronger foreign demand for goods made by North American companies is a key driver of our economy.

The composition of our society is fundamentally changing at light speed — a fact that astute organizations will view as an opportunity. For health care organizations and government agencies, providing language access enables better outcomes and increased satisfaction. For businesses, an in-language experience stands to attract and maintain a loyal customer base.

Now in our fourth decade, LanguageLine Solutions is proud to deliver language access that empowers relationships by lifting cultural barriers. We are fanatical about people understanding people, and we are passionate about seeing people smile when they are understood. We are proud that our solutions help to ensure justice, save lives, welcome newborns, and build futures.

LanguageLine is delighted to present the latest edition of *The Guide to Translation and Localization*. In addition to information about the industry, it offers insight, perspective, and critical ideas that allow organizations to harness the power of language. It delivers tips for planning and executing translation and localization projects, as well as case studies designed to illustrate key principles and strategies for success.

Our world is changing. *The Guide to Translation and Localization* makes sense of this new landscape. We are confident you will find it an invaluable tool that will help you adapt your message to new audiences.

Sincerely,

Scott W. Klein

President & CEO

LanguageLine Solutions

President's Message

The entire LanguageLine Solutions team is very excited to present the eighth edition of *The Guide to Translation and Localization*. Over the last twenty years we have distributed more than 45,000 copies of this book worldwide. Previous editions won several national awards from the Society for Technical Communication (STC), and we are often told by readers that they consider it to be the definitive source for information about translation and localization. While we welcome the accolades, our objectives in creating this guide remain unchanged: present clear, effective solutions that reduce costs, save time, and educate the marketplace about the localization process itself.

Since the last edition was published, the language services industry has evolved in dramatic fashion as the largest firms continue to absorb smaller ones. LanguageLine itself has had a front row seat to this consolidation. In late 2016, we transformed the language services industry by joining Teleperformance, the worldwide leader in outsourced omnichannel customer experience management.

Unlike other consolidations, however, this was not a "same silo" merger between competitors. Instead, the world-class solutions offered by LanguageLine and TelePerformance, respectively, are complimentary. LanguageLine created the over the phone interpretation industry more than 35 years ago and, today, is the largest sole source provider of language services (translation, localization, phone interpretation, video interpretation, and onsite interpretation) in the world. Most remarkably, our highly trained linguists facilitate more than 35,000,000 interactions every year (i.e., one new connection every second!) in more than 240 languages. No other vendor comes remotely close.

Teleperformance connects some of the biggest and most respected brands on the planet with their customers by providing customer care, technical support, customer acquisition, digital solutions, analytics, back-office, and other specialized services to ensure consistently positive customer interactions. Like LanguageLine, Teleperformance understands how the power of communication can help customers grow to their full potential.

Together, our global reach includes more than 350 offices in 74 countries throughout Europe, Asia, Africa, and North America; and our 220,000 employees interact with 38% of the world's population annually. In an increasingly interconnected world where people of many nationalities converge, LanguageLine and Teleperformance are redefining the language services industry by offering what no other LSP can: an integrated solution to meet all of an organization's language needs, in whatever modality they prefer.

As with previous editions, the eighth edition of *The Guide to Translation and Localization* is almost entirely written by LanguageLine personnel. More than thirty team members wrote sections, or provided input, comments, and technical support. As such, rather than being written in "one voice," each chapter reflects the personality of its author, allowing you to develop a feel

Scott Ludwigsen

I have worked in four very different industries: public accounting (auditor), forest products (sawmills), precious metals (refineries), and for the last 15 years, language services (translation). At some level, business is business; but this industry is different. What we do matters. By helping people communicate, we improve their lives. We help them celebrate good times; and get through bad ones. This sense of purpose permeates the culture of the LanguageLine team. It's palpable. It's amazing. I wouldn't want it any other way.

for the diversity of cultures, talents, and experience here at LanguageLine. Pictures of the contributors are scattered throughout to let you put a face to the names you will find in the acknowledgment section. Clearly this is a team effort in which we all take great pride.

For the eighth edition, we are also delighted to include a guest chapter by Kevin Cohn, SVP of Operations at Smartling. One of the most important technologies used by language service providers today are proxy tools. Smartling's translation software prioritizes process automation and intelligent collaboration so that companies can quickly and cost-effectively localize their websites, apps, and documents with minimal IT involvement. In this chapter, Kevin describes how their industry leading platform operates, and provides some great case studies on how it can accelerate time to market, and provide faster, cheaper web localization.

We are also very excited to include "ask the expert" contributions from some of the most widely respected thought leaders in the language services industry. They include: Winnie Heh, Career Advisor for Translation, Interpretation, and Localization Management at Middlebury Institute of International Studies at Monterey; Laura Brandon, Executive Director, Globalization and Localization Association (GALA); Salvatore "Salvo" Giammarresi, Head of Content & Globalization, PayPal; Florian Faes, Co-Founder & Managing Director, Slator; Jack Welde, Co-Founder & CEO, Smartling; Toos Stoker, Digital Marketing Director, TAUS; Dr. Nitish Singh, Program Leader (Global Digital Marketing), Brand2Global; and Tex Texin, Founder, Chief Architect and Xen Master, XenCraft. Thank you all for your contributions. You have made this latest edition truly special!

The Guide to Translation and Localization is designed to be an easy read that provides guidance on all aspects of the localization process. For our readers who are new to localization, we define key terms, explain the various options for translating materials, identify issues to consider when procuring localization services, describe the localization process itself, and provide many tips to control costs and improve quality. Localization veterans will find useful information on emerging trends, as well as technical discussions about software and multi-media localization.

While we invite you to read *The Guide to Translation and Localization* in its entirety, each chapter has been written to stand alone and to be read as needed. You may find, for example, that certain chapters are relevant for your marketing staff, others for your engineering staff, and yet others for your customer service or technical publications departments. Hopefully you will find all of them helpful, with useful information for everyone in your organization.

Finally, we have again provided a number of translation mistakes in our "Say What?!" sections. These are funny translations that have gone awry, and highlight the pitfalls of translations done by amateurs. We expect that you will find them to be humorous, but we also want to illustrate an important point: losing market share because your product seems "foreign" or "low quality" is not a laughing matter.

We hope you enjoy *The Guide to Translation and Localization* and find it a valuable tool for communicating with your multilingual customers and employees both in the US and throughout the world.

Sincerely,

Scott Ludwigsen

President

LanguageLine Translation Solutions

INTRODUCTION

Building a Business Case for Language Services

Language services are all about words. So naturally, let's start with some numbers.

Reach the growing U.S. non-English speaking population

 1 in 5 speaks a language other than English at home [1]

 61.7M in 2013 grown 3x in U.S. since 1980 [1]

 U.S. Hispanic market buying power $1.6T in 2018 [2]

 U.S. Asian market buying power $962B in 2018 [2]

Seize Global Online Opportunities

 Global spending power of $40T [2]

 More than 85% of the world's online population has made a purchase. [3]

 2015 online spending power is $1.5T [4]

Increase revenue and reach more buyers

 80% prefer mother tongue website purchases [5]

 85% decide to purchase when the information is in their language [5]

 72% will only buy products sold in their preferred language [5]

Provide outstanding customer service

 74% say that they're more likely to purchase the same brand again if the after-sales care is in their language. [5]

 80% desire customer care in their own language [5]

[1] U.S. Census 2013
[2] The Multicultural Economy 2013 The University of Georgia, Terry College of Business, Selig Center for Economic Growth
[3] Nielsen Global Online Survey
[4] Mediacom 2015
[5] 2014 Common Sense Advisory Report "Can't Read, Won't Buy"

While some business leaders are lukewarm about paying for professional translation services, the largest and most innovative companies invest hundreds of thousands of dollars, and in some cases tens of millions of dollars, on localization. Why? Because customers are more likely to buy a product or service when the message is presented in their native language, even if they understand the other language.

Top 10 translation bloopers

10. The lift is being fixed. During that time we regret that you will be unbearable.
    -sign in Bucharest hotel lobby

9. STOP! Drive Sideways.
    -detour sign in Japan

8. If you consider our help impolite, you should see the manager.
    -sign in an Athens hotel

7. Our wines leave you nothing to hope for.
    -on the menu of a Swiss restaurant

6. Specialist in women and other diseases.
    -doctor's office in Rome

5. Drop your pants here for best results.
    -sign at a dry cleaning store in Tokyo

4. We take your bags and send them in all directions.
    -sign at a Scandinavian airport

3. Ladies may have a fit upstairs.
    -sign at a dry cleaning store in Bangkok

2. Here speeching American.
    -sign in a Moroccan shop

1. No smoothen the lion.
    -sign in a zoo in the Czech Republic

A comprehensive language strategy will benefit you and your organization in one or more of three ways:

Accessing new markets and expanding existing markets,

Retaining current market share as demographics evolve, and

Reducing cost as a consequence of liability, non-compliance, or inefficiency.

ROI

Investing in languages pays. If your sales team says that you will be able to generate an additional $100,000 of revenue if you translate your website into five new languages and the cost will be $50,000, it makes little sense to only translate two of the five. In fact, given the 100% return on investment, it probably makes sense to translate all five languages even if you have to borrow the funds to pay for it.

Conversely, if the incremental revenue is only $50,000 and the cost to translate is $100,000, there may be no reason to engage in translation work.

Depending on the nature of your products or services, you may not have much choice about whether to localize. Many organizations engage in localization because of legal or regulatory requirements to do so; in some cases failure to localize also can prevent distribution of the product in the target market.

TIP: Always seek legal counsel regarding the implications of not localizing some or all content when selling in a new market or when offering certain types of regulated products and services to a multilingual domestic audience.

There are other reasons aside from increasing revenue you may need to localize as well. If software developers want to increase customer usability, in addition to localizing the software interface, they will need to consider localizing everything else associated with the application too. This project would include translating Help files, "read me" files, installers, legal warranties, user guides, and installation instructions as well.

Similarly, if you are going to roll out a new business system, you will probably need to translate the training materials needed to teach your global workforce how to use it. In this case, you will need to determine what languages your employees speak, and which courses they need. Finally, by choosing not to localize certain products, you run the risk of missing sales, or even worse, offending the target consumers in a new market by not providing information in their language.

The fact is that most companies and organizations are, in some way or another, facing either opportunity or dilemma as a result of today's increasingly global society.

To be sure, becoming a multilingual organization is not like learning a foreign language in your spare time. Equipping your workforce with instant, around-the-clock access to interpreters, or releasing your new software or website in two new languages is more than a side project. Like upgrading to a new business management system or hiring new employees, the decision depends on whether the potential gains justify the expense. A solutions-driven language service provider (LSP) can help you identify potential gains from expanding your language capabilities and then realize those gains in the most cost-effective way possible.

Organizations that understand and embrace the new multilingual communication paradigm will almost assuredly improve their businesses. Conversely, for those who choose to ignore it, the result may be costly.

Accessing New Markets and Expanding Existing Markets
Simply put, consumers don't buy what they don't know about.

It is nearly certain that at some point a potential consumer has seen your advertisement or even picked up your product but done nothing more because they didn't understand it. Whether you have an eye towards international markets or a subset of a domestic market, expanding your outreach to non-English speaking consumers is the only way to overcome language barriers that are artificially limiting your potential.

In fact, by not targeting Limited English Proficient (LEP) consumers, your organization may be missing out on what could be a lucrative market segment. Census data confirms that the residents of many LEP communities have higher education levels and greater net worth than their surrounding "English speaking" neighbors.

Offering your product or service in more than one language may be the differentiator your company needs to distinguish itself in a crowded market. In addition to potentially increasing both revenues and profits, your organization will gain strategic and tactical international and intercultural experience that will be invaluable in the future.

Retaining Current Market Share

Study after study confirms that consumers buy more when they are catered to in their native language. Even if you're already engaging a bilingual consumer using English, the reality is that they prefer doing business in their native language. Offering your service or information about your product in another language can help you get more out of existing customers. Moreover, customer satisfaction and retention are directly proportional to levels of language access. Consumers who cannot get the support they need in a language they understand are more likely to either stop using a service or product or switch to a provider who offers in-language support.

Reducing Cost as a Consequence of Liability, Non-compliance, Risk, or Inefficiency

Many organizations turn to LSPs for their compliance needs as well. Failing to comply with language access requirements can lead to significant costs as a result of fines and penalties. Many laws at the federal, state and local levels necessitate the use of an interpreter and translated materials. These laws affect organizations to varying degrees.

Depending on your industry, you may be more or less familiar with laws about language access. For example, US federal government agencies must abide by Clinton Executive Order 13166, requiring these agencies to provide meaningful access to services for limited English proficient speakers. In October 2011, New York Governor Andrew Cuomo issued executive order #26 for a state-wide language access policy. Cuomo's executive order, which will likely be adopted by other states, includes some of the following requirements:

> *"Executive State agencies that provide direct public services shall translate vital documents, including essential public documents such as forms and instructions provided to or completed by program beneficiaries or participants. The translation shall be in the six most common non-English languages spoken by individuals with limited-English proficiency in the State of New York, based on United States census data, and relevant to services offered by each of such agencies. Translation shall be achieved on a rolling basis to be completed no later than 365 days of the signing of this Order."*

Similar regulations exist in the health care industry. At the heart of the Affordable Care Act (ACA) is the desire to reduce costs by shifting the emphasis away from the amount of care provided and towards the quality of the care afforded. Among the financial incentives that were put in place to align the behaviors of health care providers with this goal were (1) tying Medicare reimbursements to readmission rates, and (2) issuing bonuses or penalties to providers based on patient satisfaction levels. Both are directly impacted by the translation of health care documentation.

Legal liability issues extend into nearly every sector. Tort claims arising from failure to provide spoken or written language services threaten virtually any organization. The health care industry is especially vulnerable to these risks in the form of malpractice regarding LEP patients. Product manufacturers, too, stand to lose if operation or maintenance manuals are not translated or are translated poorly.

Whether your organization is marketing heavy machinery or a medical diagnostic tool, consumers need to know how to use these machines safely and correctly. Properly translated information is essential.

For a deeper conversation about the regulatory environment in the Government, Financial Services and Health Care sectors, see Chapters 11, 12, and 13 for more information.

Saying "Yes" to Multilingual Communication

Has anyone actually heard of an organization that did not want to communicate better with their employees, customers, or constituents? Risk, aside, language access is just plain good business. Excellent communication promotes efficiency and growth. Poor communication results in inefficiency and loss. Training your LEP employees in sales strategies or customer service standards will invariably lead to improved performance and ideally, better retention of multicultural clients. Likewise, paying to train the same employees multiple times represents significant cost. Efficiently and quickly implementing changes in corporate policy across worldwide offices also requires effective multilingual communication.

In other settings, failing to communicate with multicultural patients can have a direct impact on the accuracy of their diagnosis and the effectiveness of their treatment. It is much easier and much less costly if a physician can properly communicate with a patient, and could even be the difference between life and death.

Government agencies, 911 emergency services and court systems also need language services on a daily basis. Complying with language access requirements and improving communication reduces potential liability and eliminates waste. More importantly, the ability for police officers, firemen and EMTs to communicate in multiple languages may be a matter of life and death in this vertical as well.

The Bottom Line

As globalization reshapes the world, all organizations looking to expand, secure their financial futures, or make a positive impact in the communities they serve should consider what language services can do for their enterprises. Although this may seem like an expensive or daunting proposition, the right language services partner can help you explore the various ways to tap into your communication potential.

CHAPTER 1

What are Language Services?

What exactly are language services? First-time customers may be intimidated by all the jargon they hear and might even feel as though they need a language service provider (LSP) just to decipher the jargon used by the industry.

Maybe you're wondering about odd-looking acronyms and abbreviations you have seen (like l10n, i18n, and GILT), or you're just trying to figure out what to order from your vendor. While the terminology can be overwhelming, the good news is that language services divide naturally into two basic realms: written language and spoken (or signed) language.

The Written Page

Writing is the tangible, concrete form of language; it is a physical record of ideas, thoughts, and concepts. Below are definitions of the key terms at the core of written language services.

Translation is the process of converting the text of a source language into a target language. An understanding of the context or meaning of the source language must be established in order to convey the same message in the target language. Translation is a crucial component of localization.

Localization is the process of adapting a software application, document, or website to various markets or localities so that it seems natural to that particular region. This may require a variety of steps including translating user interface text, modifying formats for numbers and dates, and replacing culturally inappropriate graphics or system design. In the abbreviation "l10n", the number 10 refers to the ten letters between the "l" and the "n."

Internationalization is the process of generalizing a product so that it can be localized into multiple languages and cultural conventions without needing to be redesigned. In the abbreviation "i18n," the number 18 refers to the eighteen letters between the "i" and the "n."

Globalization is the process of conceptualizing your product for the global marketplace so that it can be sold anywhere in the world with only minor revision. It addresses the business issues associated with launching a product globally, such as integrating localization throughout a company after proper internationalization and product design. In the abbreviation "g11n", the number 11 refers to the eleven letters between the "g" and the "n."

These four terms, often referred to collectively by the acronym *"GILT,"* are most easily understood if you visualize them as a "bull's eye" diagram. Globalization envelops the entire concept of taking your product line global. Internationalization is performed so that the product can then be localized. Finally, translation is the "base" component of the entire process as it represents the language transformation. G11n, i18n, l10n account for and help manage the cultural and technical elements of preparing your product for a new locale.

Imagine that you are a product manager for a new software application that manages sales contacts. Your product development team likely assembled comments from distributors throughout the world whose customers requested new features for your yet-to-be designed contact management software. Your marketing department has determined the global demand for this application and has developed a global branding campaign. Your design team then begins work on the look and feel of the software. Here is where internationalization comes into play. You and your team must consider the following:

- Color schemes and graphic selection that avoids offending potential customers whose beliefs and customs vary by region,
- Dialog boxes wide enough or dynamic enough to accommodate text expansion that varies by language,

The Guide to Translation and Localization

Theresa Devenport

I grew up in a small farming town where our team mascots included the Melon Pickers (for the abundance of sweet "Hearts of Gold" cantaloupes) and the Greenwave (for the rolling fields of green alfalfa). Now that I work at LanguageLine as a Sr. Project Manager, I can only chuckle at how the translation of these mascot names into other languages would turn out.

- Functionality that supports various date, time, and currency formats,
- Input and output functionality that supports all character sets and a wide range of fonts,
- Right-justified text fields to prevent expanded text from overlapping the graphics, and
- A readily adaptable user interface to allow British customers to read from left to right or Egyptian customers to read from right to left.

Taking these factors into consideration in the early stages of project planning can save enormous amounts of money and effort down the road.

Of course, designing your product with a global mindset is only the first step. Selling your contact management software to the customers in your new markets will likely require localizing the user's manual, software, help files, and user interface from English into each target language. While that may sound like a lot, the cost will be exponentially higher both before and after localization if you have not properly internationalized your content. One software manufacturer found nearly 50% of all their support costs came from helping consumers in foreign markets who could not understand English documentation.

The Spoken (or Signed) Word

Unlike the written word, speech is temporary. The words we speak exist only briefly as the sounds or shapes that make them up are articulated and transmitted. Meaning hitches itself to these signals, and that meaning is interpreted in real time by a listener as the signals themselves disappear.

Nevertheless, the same barriers we encounter with written language apply to spoken language and the need to transfer information from one language to another remains. Not surprisingly, though, the way we deal with discourse between speakers of different languages requires a different approach.

Interpretation is the conversion of spoken words from one language to another. For most people, this conjures up images of a summit between world leaders, the UN, or perhaps even a conference they have attended. For this type of interpretation, which is the most difficult of all language services, the interpreter translates the speech as it is being given so that participants can hear what is being said, as it is being said, in their native language; hence the name *simultaneous interpretation*. In contrast, the most common form of interpretation is called *consecutive interpretation*, wherein an entire thought is expressed by the speaker, the speaker pauses, and the interpreter converts the content for the target language speakers to hear.

What are Language Services?

An important characteristic of interpretation is that it is not word-for-word, but meaning-for-meaning. Qualified interpreters are not only fluent in the languages of both parties involved in an exchange, but also intimately familiar with both cultures. They also are well versed in the relevant topic(s) (health care, finance, legal, emergency service, etc.), and demonstrate superior customer service. And regardless of the language or education level of the parties needing interpretation, interpreters have the necessary vocabulary, both formal and informal, and cultural knowledge to facilitate accurate and thorough exchanges.

Onsite[SM] **interpretation** (face-to-face) is fairly self-explanatory. It requires no special technology and puts limited-English speaking individuals face to face with qualified interpreters. This type of interpreting is used most frequently in settings where direct, interpersonal communication is important. For example, many hospitals and other health care organizations employ onsite interpreters to facilitate conversations between patients and doctors. Onsite interpretation is also commonly used in professional situations such as trials, legal depositions, worker's compensation meetings, and multilingual business meetings. It is also ideal for social events like receptions, facility site visits, and guided tours. However, since it requires the physical presence of an interpreter with specific language skills, its limits are quickly apparent.

The **Over-the-Phone-Interpretation (OPI)** industry was created more than thirty years ago by LanguageLine Solutions and is the most common type of interpretation service used around the world. During over the phone interpretation, interpreters manage a three-way conversation between an organization's representative and their limited-English speaking customer. OPI's main advantage is that it is an on demand service and gives users access to interpreters for language combinations that might otherwise be impossible to find in a certain area.

This sign is a common sight in the Czech Republic, but what does it mean? In reality, the Czech means *interpretation* prohibited, and the sign is intended to discourage guided tour groups through certain neighborhoods. How many people do you think understand that, though?

Today, new technologies are enabling all sorts of exciting enhancements to traditional interpretation, including **video interpretation** and **live-chat interpretation**. The benefits of these expanded capabilities are multifold.

> <u>Video interpretation</u> is the newest emerging technology in the language services industry and combines the best elements of over the phone and onsite interpretation. With nothing more than an internet connection and a computer, iPad, or Smartphone, limited English proficient (LEP) consumers can see a live interpreter, without the cost of bringing them to your physical location. Video interpreting enables Deaf or hard of hearing patients to access American Sign Language (ASL) interpreters when they need to communicate with someone who cannot sign. In spoken language situations, video interpreting creates a more intimate setting and provides a better experience for customers and stakeholders.

> <u>Live-chat interpretation</u> is an exciting new service that combines elements of translation and interpretation to meet the growing and evolving demands driven by an increasingly global world. Anyone who has tried to access customer assistance from a website knows that almost every company now directs them to an online chat session. In fact, many companies no longer publish phone numbers for their customers to call. As the name implies, live-chat interpretation allows LEPs to utilize these services too; although in most cases, the text conversion relies on Machine Translation (see Chapters 3 and 19 for the pros and cons of "MT") rather than live interpreters.

The Final Say

Every organization's needs are different when it comes to language services. Maybe you need an interpreter three times a month. Maybe you need to translate 20,000 words of employee training material. Or maybe you need a little bit of everything. While there are many providers specializing in different language services, only a few are able to provide an integrated language access strategy that allows your multilingual audience to communicate in whatever modality they want, when they need it. In Chapter 2 we will compare and contrast the many options that are available to buyers of language services to help you make the best decision for your organization.

CHAPTER 2
I'm Ready. How Do I Get it Done?

Your organization has made the commitment to expand internationally and you're responsible for making sure that the translation of your carefully crafted English content doesn't end up reading like those laughably bad assembly instructions that we have all tried to decipher at one time or another.

For most first-timers, their initial thought may be to use a service like Google Translate because it is easy and free. But you know that is not the best option because you've skipped ahead and read Chapter 3 of this book, "Don't Just Google It." Their next thought is that a Japanese or French-speaking colleague in IT will be able to translate for them. It soon becomes apparent, however, that this endeavor far exceeds what your colleagues can do in their "free time." So how should you approach translation projects and how do you know which is the right way?

The table on the next page provides a brief summary of the most common options for translating your materials. Although this is not an exhaustive list, it should give a prospective translation buyer the information they need to make an informed decision about how to get their materials translated. As you will see, you have many options for translating from Albanian to Zulu, and everywhere else in between.

Which Option is Right for Me?

It should never be apparent to the end users that the content they are reading or the product they are holding has been translated into their language from another. A properly localized product should have the look and feel of having been created specifically for the target market.

If this is your goal, you can eliminate a few of the options in the chart below. In most cases, using machine translations or non-professional resources such as bilingual family members, acquaintances or co-workers will not produce the quality you desire. Only a highly-skilled professional translator can provide polished translations that are consistently accurate and stylistically natural.

Isn't it Easier for My Overseas Office to Do It?

You might be tempted to use your overseas office to localize your product. They speak the language after all, so it should be easy, right? The temptation is even greater if you have an in-country subsidiary or distributor offering to do the translation for you. While it is true that these options may be the best solution in some cases, it can also lead to other problems:

- Less control from headquarters,
- Difficulty in project coordination and communication,
- Unauthorized changes to the content,
- Risks to schedule, and
- Incorrect translations (they are likely not professional translators).

If nothing else, the time zones will be an issue because you may wait an entire day to communicate about a single subject, which could delay project launches. Also, when you send your materials to an overseas office or distributor, you create an opportunity for them to modify both your content and message. The in-country team may have different priorities from your US-based team, resulting in changes to branding, use of terminology, and perhaps features that have been disabled or removed from the US version.

Unfortunately, you might not become aware of these modifications until a problem arises or someone translates the in-country translations back to English. One client that took this route and was alarmed to discover that their foreign office had deleted all contact information for in-country technical support and instead substituted a comment instructing the consumer to contact the reseller with any problems!

The Guide to Translation and Localization

What Are My Options?

	Language Service Provider **LanguageLine Solutions®**	Individual Translator(s)	Crowdsourcing	Online Machine Translation	Overseas distributor or other partner	Bilingual Employee	Acquaintance or family friend
	An organization dedicated to providing a broad range of linguistic, technological, design, and consultation services in multiple languages	An independent contractor who specializes in one language	A community based (usually online) approach where work is split, but translation efforts are uncoordinated	Google Translate or similar	Foreign distributor, agent or representative	Someone in your company who speaks the target language	Someone you know who happens to speak or has studied the target language
Features							
Professional Translators and Linguists	YES	YES	MAYBE	NO	NO	NO	NO
Full Privacy and Data Protection	YES	NO	NO	NO	NO	NO	NO
Rigorous, standardized QA process	YES	NO	NO	NO	NO	NO	NO
Additional support services, e.g. engineering and DTP	YES	NO	NO	NO	NO	NO	NO
Access to subject matter experts	YES	YES	NO	NO	YES	YES	NO
(Virtually) unlimited capacity to meet any timeline demands	YES	NO	YES	YES	NO	NO	NO
Easy updates	YES	NO	NO	NO	NO	NO	NO
Full-service Project Management	YES	NO	NO	NO	NO	NO	NO
Current translation and translation management tools	YES	YES	NO	NO	NO	NO	NO
Cost	$$$	$$-$$$	$	FREE	$-$$	$	$

I'm Ready. How Do I Get it Done?

Horror stories such as these can be avoided by choosing the right people for the right job. In most cases, the best result is obtained by hiring a professional localization resource for translation and then using your in-country representatives to assist with "terminology list" development and a final review of the localized content. This strategy enables you to coordinate all localization efforts centrally, while encouraging your overseas partners to buy in on the final product.

Can't I Just Hire Individual Translators?

Your final choice is between hiring individual translators or a full-service localization vendor to manage all of your localization efforts. The considerations here involve time, quality, budget, and the need for value-added services. Do you have the time and staff to hire and manage individual translators, and assess the quality of their results?

If you desire to manage the project on your own without the assistance of an LSP, the use of locally-based, single-language translators can be an effective solution for very small projects with one target language. This option works best when translating from English into a common language (so that it is easy to find a linguist), the formatting is simple (such as Microsoft Word), subsequent updates are unlikely, timelines are flexible, and projects are infrequent. As the volume of material or the number of target languages increases, the limitations of this approach will become increasingly obvious. Keep in mind that with single-language translators, your management and coordination load will increase exponentially as the number of target languages grows.

In comparison, a full-service LSP can provide you with all the resources necessary to receive high-quality translations on time and on budget, reducing your need to be involved in the day-to-day execution of the project. When aggressive timelines are required, they have the ability to build and manage large teams of translators. They are also able to perform both linguistic and functional QA to ensure the translation is correct. And, they probably have an engineering team that can work with, and extract text from, any file type. Perhaps most significantly, most firms will be able to use sophisticated localization tools, discussed later in this book, that will yield significant savings on future projects.

As you consider all of the available options, let your project goals lead you to the best solution.

> トイレを綺麗に ご 使用下さい。
>
> Please use a toilet finely.
>
> 漂亮地请使用厕所
>
> 화장실을 에쁘게 사용해 주십시오
>
> 鹿 苑 寺

A bathroom sign in Japan

Chapter 3
Don't Just Google It

A popular question these days when it comes to translation and localization is: Why can't I just use Google Translate?

Google Translate is indeed a fascinating tool. It puts the ability to translate to and from over one hundred languages at the fingertips of millions across the globe, and it has put machine translation (MT) in the public spotlight in an unprecedented way. Whether you're talking about Google Translate, Microsoft Skype or an even more sophisticated system, MT is reshaping the language services industry. Not only is it instantaneous and much lower in cost (if not free), in most cases the output is good enough to at least understand the gist of most documents.

As almost anyone who has used these tools can attest, however, the output often has significant shortcomings. Given all of the amazing things that modern technology can do, why isn't MT output better than it is? After all, the first successful MT experiment was conducted in 1954 when scientists at Georgetown University translated more than 60 Russian sentences into English. At the time, the scientific community was convinced that the machine translation "problem" would be solved in three to five years. Flash-forward years later: W have self-driving cars, 3-D printing, and robotic surgery, and yet MT is wildly inconsistent. Why is that?

The main reason these free tools struggle when translating from one language to another is that language is hard. The same words can often have completely different meanings.

A sign in Bulgaria

As the examples on this page illustrate, language is perplexing, and to understand it and use it correctly is a highly nuanced skill. Whether in written or spoken form, many factors come into play beyond the actual words or phrases being used: overall context, tone of voice, inflection, pausing, body language (if visible), figures of speech, and a host of background cultural factors all play a part in deriving the actual clear and accurate meaning from a word or phrase. Increased stress and other emotions can cloud the situation even further.

Automated translation apps simply can't account for all these subtleties, with the end result sometimes being comical. But when a situation is serious, a comical misunderstanding can be frustrating or even dangerous. That's why a professional translator or interpreter remains the preferred means of language access when you can't risk inaccuracy.

20 Reasons Why English is Hard to Learn!

- The bandage was wound around the wound.
- The farm was used to produce produce.
- The dump was so full that it had to refuse more refuse.
- We must polish the Polish furniture.
- He could lead if he would get the lead out.
- The soldier decided to desert his dessert in the desert.
- Since there is no time like the present, he thought it was time to present the present.
- A bass was painted on the head of the bass drum.
- When shot at, the dove dove into the bushes.
- I did not object to the object.
- The insurance was invalid for the invalid.
- There was a row among the oarsmen about how to row.
- They were too close to the door to close it.
- The buck does funny things when does are present.
- A seamstress and a sewer fell down into a sewer line.
- The wind was too strong to wind the sail.
- After a number of injections my jaw got number.
- Upon seeing the tear in the painting I shed a tear.
- I had to subject the subject to a series of tests.
- The accountant at the music store records records of the records.

From the I18n Guy.com website

A professional linguist should be not just bilingual, but bicultural as well. They're capable of not just providing a word-for-word literal regurgitation of vocabulary from one language to another, but of actually transmitting the intended thoughts and meanings—with all their nuances—from one language to another. In the end, only a translator can put the same thought into your translation as you put into the original text.

Google Translate and other tools like it do still serve an important purpose: they help people communicate. So even when the results aren't perfect, they enable people to ask for help, get directions to a restaurant, or understand the gist of an article or email. These tools are not, however, designed to localize a website, technical manual, or marketing collateral. Even Google acknowledges this. In fact, Google is one of the very largest buyers of *human* translation services in the world!

Finally and perhaps most importantly, companies that may be considering using Google Translate to localize their proprietary information need to carefully evaluate the level of security they are willing to accept. According to their official terms and conditions (at the time of this writing), Google acquires ownership of any information that has been translated through the Translate tool. Depending on the nature of the content being translated, this presents any number of privacy risks, as well as copyright risks. Be careful when using this service for any confidential or proprietary information. Inadvertent violations of privacy laws can be costly.

Take for example the $43B Norwegian oil company called Statoil who learned this the hard way. They used Translate.com, a free online tool, to translate notices of dismissal, plans of workforce reductions and outsourcing, passwords, code information, and contracts, only to find the translation all of this sensitive material was later discoverable via a basic Google search.

At LanguageLine, one of the most common questions we hear is: "Maybe not today but isn't Google Translate eventually going to put you out of business?" Our answer is always the same. We're very excited about the great strides that Google Translate and other similar tools have made in recent years. Here's why:

Every business should be excited about technology and how it can be harnessed and deployed to improve the products and services offered to its clients. The companies that don't get excited and stay in touch with evolving technology tend to be the ones who suffer. (Think Kodak way back when digital photography was new.)

The very fact that the public is increasingly interacting with language translation and interpretation technologies means multilingual awareness in our society is on the rise.

What's more exciting to us is how the technology and the human element can work together so harmoniously right now! In Chapter 19, we explain how commercial MT tools work and how, when paired with human editors (known as "post-editors"), they can increase the amount of content translated while decreasing the cost to do so. As MT technology continues to improve and spread further into everyday life, we expect that these tools will continue to make it easier to connect and communicate. At the same time, it is also clear that when critical accuracy is required, it's not yet good enough to just Google it.

Alex Macnab

I was born in England and grew up in Texas, raised by my British Mother and Texan Father. As a dual US and UK citizen I've spoken two English languages all my life! I started work with LanguageLine in the London office and moved back to Texas in 2009. When I'm not travelling around the US consulting with customers on translation and localization best practices, I enjoy photography, watching Rugby, and spending time with my wife and two kids.

CHAPTER 4
Planning a Successful Project

If your research has led you this far, it is more than likely that your project or program will require the help of a professional language service provider (LSP). After reading *The Guide to Translation and Localization*, you will be in a great position to begin discussing your project with an LSP and refining the scope of the work required. Not surprisingly, timeline, cost, and quality will be the driving factors in coming up with a solution, and you must set accurate and realistic goals for each of these variables prior to planning your project.

During analysis and planning, keep in mind that localization is a group effort. Most projects are relatively complex affairs that require numerous specialized resources, each functioning to provide unique and closely interrelated contributions. Each of these factors has a significant impact on how much time it will take and how much it will cost.

Finding the right solution starts with asking some "big picture" questions:

- What is your long-term globalization strategy?
- How is your company positioned? Is it a market leader or a specialty supplier; top-of-the line standard-setter or a low-cost alternative; custom manufacturer or a commodity production; high-quality provider or a low-quality solution?

Other basic questions that are important to answer are:

- Which products and components will you localize?
- What target markets and languages do you need?
- What are the legal, regulatory, liability, and commercial requirements in the target market(s)?
- What is your timeline?
- What is your budget?
- What level of quality and consistency will you need?
- What is the likelihood and extent of on-going future updates?
- How often will you have new products for localization?
- Are there engineering and functionality considerations?
- Are there specific requirements or guidelines that need to be incorporated into the process?
- Are the source formats compatible with the languages targeted for localization? If not, will conversion options be considered?
- If there are video elements, is voice-over required? If so, what are the gender requirements and audio specifications? Will the audio be timed to a video?
- If the final product is an interactive website or application, how much functionality testing will be required? Are test scripts available, or will they need to be developed prior to testing?

With so many considerations to evaluate, the localization process may seem daunting. Fortunately, localization of virtually any component is straightforward with good planning and the right partner.

Diana Joyce

Our printed words come in all shapes and sizes—big and small, left to right or right to left, singular or plural, with glyphs and accents, in Asian characters or Roman alphabet or Cyrillic script. They are so central to who we are that without them we have lost our connection.

Guiding a team that makes them all fit on one page is brilliant!

Plan Early

There is an old carpenter's saying: "Measure twice, cut once." In other words, plan carefully and early for localization. For example, if your documentation includes 20 screen captures from the software user interface (UI), the UI should be localized before the documentation so that the terminology that is frozen and translated in the UI can be propagated to the documentation and/or help files.

When tight timelines require that UI and documentation localization occur simultaneously, aggressive localization schedules may still be possible. Because these projects frequently involve the translation of thousands of words, vendors form teams of linguists to work on both components at the same time. At some point in the schedule, after the UI is frozen, time is allocated to allow the documentation to "catch up" so that references to buttons, menus, and other items in the text of the documentation match the terminology used in the UI. Fortunately, other components such as training materials and web content can usually wait until the bulk of the product localization is complete. After all, end users can't be trained until you have something on which to train them!

One Language at a Time or All at Once?

Many international companies prefer to roll out new products to all of their markets in a simultaneous or "simship" release. Although such releases are a goal of some multinationals, they are not a commercial priority for everyone.

A simultaneous release poses two main challenges for localization. First, in order for a company to release source and localized products at the same time, localization generally needs to begin while the source is still under development. This means that each last minute change to the UI, online help, or other documentation must also be incorporated by the localization team. As you can imagine, such "stops and starts" make configuration management more complicated and the project more expensive.

Given these challenges, consider an iterative development life cycle where your localization vendor is provided with the "alpha" or "beta" version of the software. Later, when the product is "functionally complete," the vendor can finalize the translations. This approach means a little more work, but everything can be finished for a "simship." Alternatively, if you choose a delayed release—localizing your components as they are needed—you can lay the groundwork with your vendor so that each component is "ready to roll" through the production process on your signal.

The second main challenge involves managing localization team complexity and resources. Depending on the word count, timeline, and number of languages, your localization vendor may need to assemble teams of translators, copy editors, and proofreaders to translate the content. There may also be several teams of desktop publishers to lay out each page; two, three, four, or more quality assurance reviewers to inspect the work and, for technology projects, several localization engineers to process and prepare the files for each step. Coordinating all of this activity requires one or more project managers. At LanguageLine Solutions, we have delivered large rollouts to 30+ countries that required a team of more than 100 professionals! When qualifying a localization vendor, make sure they have the resources and experience to handle your project.

Getting an Estimate

After compiling a list of potential vendors, you'll want to hear what they can do for you.

As you begin your discussions with vendors, you may find that you have many more questions than answers. Undoubtedly, you will be asked to clearly articulate your requirements and provide electronic source files for the vendors to analyze.

This stage is all about exchanging information. What information does your vendor need? What information do you want back? Depending on the size of your project, you even may consider following a formal RFI (request for information), RFP (request for proposal) or RFQ (request for quote) process. Remember, assumptions represent risk for both you and the vendors. So, the more information you provide and the clearer and more concise your instructions, the more accurate the estimate and more realistic the project plan will be in return.

To help differentiate between vendors, many companies ask for a sample translation as part of the bidding process. This can be a useful tool if your materials are highly technical and you want to ensure that the localization provider is qualified to handle the translations with linguists that have the appropriate subject matter expertise. A word of caution: Since localization providers want to make a good impression, they will most likely use their best linguist to translate your sample. Unfortunately, it does not necessarily follow that the same linguist will be available (or utilized) if the vendor is awarded the work.

Asking for references also can be a fantastic way to evaluate and compare potential vendors. As with sample translations, you will almost assuredly be provided with contacts who will give positive feedback, so your objective should be to get a feel for the style and strengths of each vendor. From there, you can determine which one will be the best fit for your company.

Start by asking for companies whose projects were similar in size, scope, and type to yours. Then, when speaking with the references, ask them to describe their experience working with the vendor. Was the experience positive? How long did the project(s) take? Was it completed on time? How was the customer service? Find out how long the references have worked with the vendor.

Reliability and long-term consistency will be important factors in your selection.

ASK AN EXPERT:

What's the next largest area of growth in this industry?

Winnie Heh, Career Advisor for Translation, Interpretation, and Localization Management at Middlebury Institute of International Studies at Monterey:

Commercial application of MT in repetitive and limited domain applications. Linguistic QA personnel who are not translators per se, but are native speakers with excellent command of the languages. They will work in an environment of quick turn-around time.

The Guide to Translation and Localization

Bill Kelter

I didn't have helicopter parents. By the time I came around, they were simply too exhausted (having seven kids will do that). I got to scavenge much of my education from George Carlin records and the pages of National Lampoon. Many trips to the principal's office notwithstanding, out of my ill-mannered youth came a fascination with written communication that never left me—from the English of my leisure to the hundreds of languages that our team works with every day. The written word informs, persuades, and entertains; it looks as cool on the page as it does in neon light, and it might be the only truly infinite resource on our planet.

Selecting a Vendor

Unless you provide a template with your instructions, you will likely find that each localization provider has a slightly different way of presenting their quote to you. Some vendors will respond with a great deal of information detailing the specific tasks they propose to perform, the amount of effort that is required, and a business case for why they are the best choice to perform the work. Others may only submit minimal detail.

As described more fully in Chapters 5 and 6, the most critical differences between vendors are:

- The number of linguistic and QA steps they plan to perform,
- The qualifications and locations of their translators,
- The qualifications and locations of all other resources, and
- The tools they plan to use.

Some vendors will translate the content in one step and send it back to you. Others will have an established multi-step process that incorporates comprehensive reviews by one or more additional translators.

These differences can have a huge impact on cost and quality. So how do you choose between competing proposals when one vendor's estimate is 20% higher for what amounts to 50% more effort? Similarly, how much is it worth to you if one vendor uses college students to perform the translation while another only employs full-time, professional linguists?

Obtain the best value for your dollar by making an *apples-to-apples* comparison, but be forewarned: This is easier said than done. Standardizing localization estimates can be difficult and time-consuming. As with most things in life, you get what you pay for, and localization is no exception. Take the time to investigate each vendor's services thoroughly. Begin by asking a potential vendor these questions:

- *What subject matter and industry experience do you have?*
- *How do you qualify your linguists?*
- *Who would manage my project and where is the project manager be located?*
- *What process would you follow?*
- *If required, would you be willing and do you have any experience staffing a project manager onsite at the client's location?*
- *How often would I receive status reports on my project and what information would be in them?*
- *Who would be my primary contact during the project?*
- *Do you use state-of-the-art localization tools and, if so, which ones?*
- *When analyzing my electronic source files, do you calculate leveraging?*
- *How do you charge for repetitions, fuzzy matches, and unique text?*
- *Will you create a TM (translation memory database) and will I own it?*

- *How many projects like mine have you managed before?*
- *Can I speak with your previous clients about their experiences?*
- *How many linguistic steps will you perform?*
- *What is your quality assurance process?*
- *How would you develop and maintain a terminology list specific to my project and/or industry?*
- *What is your process for incorporating changes from our in-country review? Do you charge extra for this, and if so, how are those costs determined?*
- *Would my in-country team be able to speak directly with your linguists if necessary?*
- *How would changes be handled during the course of a project?*
- *What is your record for delivering on time?*
- *Is your estimate firm or is it subject to change?*

A qualified localization vendor should be able to provide an estimate that is comprehensive, accurate, and clearly defined. The table on the next page offers a sample pricing structure covering various services and how they might be billed.

Selecting the right localization partner is a critical component to the overall success of your expansion into new international or multi-lingual markets. The value of developing a long-term partnership cannot be overemphasized. Such a relationship provides a means for the localization team to learn about your company, constituents, and products, and to understand your requirements and expectations inside and out. Often this results in improved workflows, shorter timelines, and lower costs for you. The better your partner understands you and your product line, the more smoothly the localization process can proceed, and the more effectively project management and communication protocols can be fine-tuned. The long-term relationship between you and your localization provider is, ultimately, the best way to achieve cost-effective, high-quality work for each and every project.

ASK AN EXPERT:

What does quality mean?

Laura Brandon, GALA Executive Director

Quality is in the eye of the beholder. We see many companies choosing to go for "good enough" translations to save on time and budget. What matters to an automotive company is different than a medical device manufacturer, of course, so the important thing is that vendors and their clients mutually agree to the *expected* level of quality and how they will measure it.

The Guide to Translation and Localization

Project Type	Task	How it is billed
All Projects	Project management	Typically 10-15% of the project costs
	Translation, new text	Per word (usually a minimum charge if <250 words)
	Translation, fuzzy matched text	Per word, normally less than full word rate
	Translation, 100% matched or repetitive text	Per word, normally less than full word rate
	Copyediting	Per word or per hour (usually a minimum charge if <950 words)
	Proofreading (documentation) or online review (software or web)	Per word or per hour (usually a minimum charge if <2,000 words)
	Glossary/terminology list development	Per term or per hour
	Translation memory creation, administration, and updating	Per hour
	File treatments/file prep	Per hour
Documentation	Desktop publishing	Per hour or per page
	Graphic design	Per hour or per graphic
	PDF creation (Print or Functional)	Per hour or per page
	Quality assurance (QA)	Per hour
Software, website, & online help	Desktop publishing	Same as for documentation
	Help generation & QA	Per hour
	Engineering	Per hour
	Functional testing	Per hour
	Graphics and screen captures	Per hour
Voice-over	Voice talent	Per hour (usually a minimum charge if <2 hours)
	Studio time (audio recording, editing, archiving)	Per hour (usually a minimum charge if <2 hours)
Transcription	Conversion of audio to a written script	Per minute of recorded audio. Dependent on number of speakers, language(s), audio quality and level of transcription detail required.

Chapter 5

Quality: Every Buyer Wants It and Every Vendor Sells It, but What is It?

If you have ever attended a language industry trade show, one of the first things you will notice is that almost every exhibitor says that they provide high quality translations. Can this really be true? And if so, what exactly is a high quality translation? Most people will probably agree that "quality" is a subjective concept. And if they have ever purchased these services, it is pretty certain they'll tell you that some vendors are better than others. If they're correct, then it can't be true that every translation company provides high quality.

The difficulty of defining a "high quality" translation becomes apparent when you examine the two basic approaches that clients tend to use to do so. The first is decidedly more objective and is based on whether the translation says everything the source says ... and doesn't include things that aren't in the source.

The second not only measures what the translation says but also how well it's said. The concept of what's "good" or "bad," however, is not only subjective, but is dependent on a set of preferences that probably existed before the translation was done. In other words, you're not really comparing the target language to its source as much as you are comparing the target to a pre-conceived idea of what "good Spanish" (for example) sounds like to you. If stylistic preferences are important to your team, they need to be discussed with your vendor *before* translation starts.

Translation Quality is Multifaceted

At LanguageLine, we believe that the benchmark for translation quality should be set by your needs: there is no one-size-fits-all solution when it comes to translation and localization. The process for translating a simple email (so you can understand what your Japanese colleague is saying) should not be the same as what's required when translating the user manual for a nuclear power plant. Yet, in either case, you should expect quality.

Once your needs and intentions are clear, getting the right quality is dependent on two primary factors:

- *the skill and expertise of the linguists who perform the translations, and*
- *the number of additional "Quality Assurance" steps performed by your vendor (i.e., the "process" or "workflow" that they use to execute your project).*

To ensure that you get the right level of quality on your project, and that you don't pay for more than you need, there are many factors your language service provider (LSP) should consider and questions they should ask when deciding what workflow would be best for you. Some of the more common ones include:

- *Will the translated content be customer facing, or will it only be used internally?*
- *Will it have a long shelf life (and be seen by lots of people over an extended period), or will it only be used once and have a limited distribution?*
- *Do you need a website, eLearning, or software translated? Or is the content basic documentation?*
- *If documentation, how complex are the source files? Are they simple Word documents, or is it a high-gloss brochure that was created in InDesign and features embedded graphics?*
- *How difficult is the source content? What is the reading level? Are subject matter experts (SMEs) required? The SME could be a doctor or engineer, or simply someone who lives in the locale.*

The Guide to Translation and Localization

Cristina Tacconi

I was born in Italy but I have spent half of my life here in the USA.
I still call Italy "home" but I love my "other" home almost as much and it feels very special to me to be part of two worlds and two cultures. I have raised my two sons bilingual and it is my hope that they will continue to enjoy and appreciate the unique contributions of multicultural education and experience.
That is probably why after about twenty years I still love working in the business of languages and I feel very fortunate to be surrounded by team members who share the same dedication.
What is the secret? Besides loving the sound and visual aspect of many different languages, we are just passionate (someone would say crazy ...) about making things right and eliminating every error we can find.
In the QA Department we make sure that all our projects are reviewed through a "post translation" assessment which ensures that the layout and visual aspect of our deliverables are as close as possible to the original documents. We look at every page, every line and every word before we send our projects out the door and we are proud to offer this high quality service to all our clients.

- *How do you position yourself in the marketplace? Are you the low cost option, or do you offer a premium product at a premium price?*
- *Is an accurate translation good enough, or does the final deliverable need to be highly polished?*

The last question your vendor should ask is, "Which of the following is most important to you?"

- *How long will it take?*
- *How much will it cost?*
- *How good does it need to be?*

It's probably obvious that no matter how good your vendor may be, you can't have the best quality, at the lowest price, in the shortest time. You can definitely have one of the three, and in some cases two of the three, but never all of them on the same project at the same time.

To illustrate how the answers to these questions could impact the workflow or process that is used on your project, let's look at some real-world situations.

CASE 1: One growing sector in the translation marketplace is "eDiscovery" for corporate law offices. The challenge with eDiscovery projects is that law firms may receive tens of thousands of documents with millions of words in a foreign language that may or may not be relevant to their case. Does it really make sense to have a Translator, then an Editor, and finally a Proofreader (often referred to as a TEP or "3-step" process), translate each file? The likely answer is no, given that you don't even know which, if any, of those documents will be needed for the case. For this type of project, basic machine translation with no human post-editing afterwards is probably good enough because the attorneys just need to have a general idea of what each document says and determine if it's relevant to their case. Only the documents that are deemed pertinent will then need human translation. Because they may be used in a court, the resulting translations will have to be accurate, but not highly polished and eloquent. So in this case, a "1-step" machine translation on everything, followed by "2-step" translation for a subset of documents in which the first linguist translates the document and then a second linguist edits or reviews the work of the first, is probably good enough. Most likely, these translations will not need much formatting either.

CASE 2: Most organizations have a broad range of translation needs. The IT Department might want the website translated. The Marketing Department may have advertising content. And the Claims Department might need to translate insurance forms that are submitted by limited English proficient (LEP) claimants.

For most LSPs, this type of project diversity is not a big deal. The LSP will adapt accordingly and probably use a different workflow for each department's needs. For example, the website is the "face" of the organization and may be seen by hundreds of thousands of potential customers. An ideal workflow would be to have it translated and edited, and then given to localization engineers to complete a "build" before a third translator performs an online review of the entire website in order to see the same things a user will. The marketing content has undoubtedly been highly wordsmithed to convey a carefully crafted message and, like the website, is also customer facing. In this case, the LSP will likely use highly experienced translators who specialize in marketing content. The goal here is to avoid literal translations and, instead, convey a concept ... which often needs to be adapted or changed completely from one country to another. Lastly, the claim forms are only going to be seen by the claims processor, who just needs to know what they say. A basic "2-step" translation where the translator also formats as he or she works and the "review" is a quick check for accuracy will almost always be good enough.

CASE 3: The flexibility described in the previous case is often not available to government agencies, which are usually required to issue a formal tender and go out to bid. The resulting contracts tend to be very explicit and specify the exact services the winning firm is to perform (e.g., 2-steps, 3-steps, DTP, QA, etc.). This presents a challenge for both the agency and the LSP since the materials they need translated usually cover a wide spectrum:

Signage – public facing, but usually very simple

Public assistance forms – public facing with a long shelf life; need to be accurate, but not eloquent

Completed public assistance forms – internal use only; just need to know what it says

Public health announcements – public facing, but often used only once; just need to be accurate

Health and safety brochures – public facing and often widely distributed with a long shelf life; also common to have complex graphics and be highly stylized. Usually requires full TEP with multiple rounds of formatting and QA.

Clearly, a one size fits all solution does not work, but the contracts they put in place provide the LSP with little flexibility. Hiring agencies must also figure out how to differentiate between competing bidders. Translation is not a commodity, so how can they be certain the vendor they pick will deliver the quality they want?

CASE 4: No area of translation has changed as much over the last 10 years as training materials. Back then, almost all training was instructor lead (ILT) and localizing training content meant translating Excel, Word, and PowerPoint files. Today, most training content is delivered online (called "eLearning") using sophisticated Learning Management Systems. This means that rather than translating basic lesson documents using a straight-forward 2-step or 3-step workflow, LSPs need to perform a combination of software and multimedia localization.

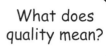

ASK AN EXPERT:

What does quality mean?

Winnie Heh, Career Advisor for Translation, Interpretation, and Localization Management at Middlebury Institute of International Studies at Monterey

On time delivery and the level of linguistic accuracy and style that match the purpose of the work.

Diana Warnock

Language shapes perception.

Perception shapes reality.

Reality is social construction, primarily built with language.

Humans are the only species having the capcities to communicate thus.

As a desktop publisher, I have opportunities to see our differences and commonalities; I believe language is the bridge across economic & cultural disparities to global nonviolence & peace.

Companies that invest in eLearning do so to make the content available on demand, usually for an extended period of time. In other words, the translated versions will have a long shelf life and, at large companies, will potentially be seen by many people. In contrast, ILT is often a one-time event, and the translations will never be used again. And, if the audience for the instructor-led-training consists of internal employees rather than customers, the translations probably don't need to be perfect. So long as the attendees understand the material, an okay translation may be good enough.

When translating training materials, it is especially important to determine how good the materials need to be to accomplish your objectives. Do they need to be highly polished and perfect, or just good enough to understand? A second question to address is how much of the content actually needs to be translated? For ILT, is it just what participants will see, or do you need to localize instructor notes as well? Similarly, if your eLearning has multimedia, will adding subtitles to the video suffice or do you prefer to have your vendor sync a Chinese audio tract, for example, to the existing video? In some cases you may even want to film new video with native actors. Whatever option you select for your eLearning project, you will need a vendor with strong engineering capabilities. Since most LSPs do not actually employ localization engineers, be sure to shop around for one that does.

Some Translators are Better Than Others

As the preceding examples illustrate, workflows clearly matter—but who does the work matters even more. Just as some people can write better than others (or sing, dance, play golf, throw darts, or solve math problems), some translators are better than others, too. This can be a function of skill, experience, or both. But make no mistake: Translation is not a commodity and not all translators are equal.

Less talented translators tend to be less expensive, which is why many translation firms hire them. It is also the reason that many LSPs are based in college towns. Unfortunately, in addition to being less experienced (if for no other reason, simply due to their age), they are often non-native speakers. But most importantly, they are college students! When they have to choose between going to class, studying for a test, going out with their friends, or meeting your deadline, which one takes priority?

In comparison, now consider a ten year veteran who is a full time professional translator, with advanced degrees, and certifications from organizations such as the American Translators Association. This subject matter expert has also been rigorously screened and tested for their linguistic competence, perhaps background checked and drug screened, and is a native speaker of the target language. Is there any doubt as to who is more likely to produce the best translation?

You Get What You Pay For

Most buyers of translation services understand that if they hire a less experienced or less skilled translator to save a few dollars, there is a pretty good chance that their translated deliverable will not be as good as what they would have received from a better linguist. They also assume that if they hire a really good translator, they will get a really good translation. In most cases, this will be true, but if you apply too much pressure on "very good" translators to accept a lower or discounted rate, most will simply do less polishing so that they can translate faster and accept more projects (thereby allowing them to make up the difference in income). Conceptually, this is no different than when you craft a memo or write a letter in English. For most people, their first draft is not as good as the version they return to three or four times to polish and refine. Translation is no different. So after you get done patting yourself on the back for squeezing an extra penny from a linguist, realize that in doing so you may have impacted the quality of the translation you will receive.

Quality Assurance – Check it once. Check it twice. Then Check it Again

When considering the quality you need and the appropriate process to achieve that quality, one of the first decisions is whether your project will be classified as Document Translation or Localization. Every LSP defines these terms differently, but typically, the core difference is that document translation projects are less complex and will need fewer linguistic and quality assurance steps. In contrast, websites, eLearning, and software need three full linguistic steps, require engineering specialists, and multiple rounds of QA. These kinds of projects are usually considered localization projects. Many vendors specialize in one or the other, but a few can (or want to) handle both types of projects.

Ultimately though, it's not the sheer *number* of steps performed that dictates the translation quality you get. While this is still a major factor, the additional value of each step is only as good as the linguist behind it. Simply going through the motions of performing multiple steps will not necessarily yield higher quality, and it can even backfire. For example, adding a cheap but unqualified (e.g., amateur, non-native) linguist to your workflow for the sake of increasing the number of steps may actually cause more work, take more time, and increase quality risks since other linguists will have to clean up the unqualified person's mistakes. Moreover, even if all of the linguists you have lined up are qualified, you must give each enough time to actually do their work well and add value. So if you only have enough time and or money for a 2-step process, there won't be any gains from forcing a 3-step process through in the same amount of time, or for the same price.

Translation Buyers Have an Impact on Quality Too

High-quality translations aren't just a function of which LSP you hire and what process they follow. There several ways that buyers of translation services can improve the quality of the translations they receive.

As discussed in Chapter 4, plan ahead and give your vendor enough time to do the job right. When time is in short supply, LSPs have two basic ways to complete your project faster:

Cut the number of quality assurance steps. This could mean fewer translation steps (e.g., "2-steps" instead of "3-steps"); using statistical sampling to only proofread some of the content rather than all of it; performing fewer DTP passes; or eliminating any of the other QA steps they usually do.

Build a bigger translation team. Most experts agree that, on average, professional linguists translate between 2,000 and 2,500 words per day. Although it's theoretically possible to take a 10 page document and give each page to a different translator to get it all done in one day, it is always best to use the smallest number of linguists as possible if consistency of terminology or voice are important to you.

Dianne Ellis

One of my favorite things in the world is being an aunt. And, any way you say it, "Kumusta ka na po, tita Dianne", "Salut tante Dianne", "Ciao, zia Dianne!", or "Hallo tante Dianne", hearing those sweet voices say "Hi Aunt Dianne" just warms my heart every time.

Also, if you have stylistic or terminological preferences, work with your vendor before the project starts to create a Style Guide that details the "rules" the translators should follow when working on your project. As discussed in Chapter 7 of this book, these usually include desired tone (formal vs. conversational); a list of terms that should not be translated; rules for capitalization, spelling of numbers, punctuation, and accent marks; and other dos and don'ts. A terminology list of approved translations for key terms is also recommended.

Finally, integrating a formal review of draft deliverables into the workflow by your in-country employees will add value to any localization project. This step, which is often referred to as ICR, or In-Country Review, accomplishes several things: prior to release, it puts the files in front of an industry expert with first-hand knowledge of the material; it creates an opportunity to gain buy-in from your international partners; and it can increase your confidence in the quality of your vendor's work. Ideally, the reviewer(s) you designate for ICR were involved in or briefed on any preliminary efforts to develop glossaries or terminology lists. They should have the same information you gave your vendor at the start of the project so that stylistic differences at this late stage do not result in costly revisions. See Chapter 9 of this book for more information on ICR reviews.

Conclusion

When buying translation and localization services, it is important to remember two key points. First, not all projects require the same level of quality. Second, different workflows produce different results. As a buyer of these services, you shouldn't have to tell your vendor how to do their job, but if you don't communicate your preferences, needs, priorities, and expectations, it's extremely unlikely that you will get you what you want from your vendor.

Fortunately, the best LSPs will ask questions and present you with options for how to complete your project. Still, it's important that you recognize the relationship between process and quality before you shop for vendors. After all, behind every quote is a process. You should be prepared to ask (and understand the answers to) these questions:

What services are you getting for the price you've been quoted?

Are they selling you more than you need?

Are they doing enough for that price to meet your needs?

Understanding how process impacts quality will help you make apples-to-apples comparisons between quotes from different vendors, and it will also reveal whether your potential vendor's idea of a high-quality solution is the same as yours.

CHAPTER 6
Process is the Key to Success

Technology has fundamentally changed the way we communicate with each other, and to remain competitive in the global marketplace (or perhaps more appropriately, the online marketplace) organizations must engage their stakeholders through a variety of media in whatever language they speak, via every modality they offer. Among the more common are:

- *Company websites* (often featuring animated or interactive intros, videos, and other multimedia tools)
- *Graphic User Interfaces* (GUIs)
- *User manuals*
- *Service manuals*
- *Online help*
- *eLearning* and other training material
- *Virtual storefronts*
- *CD versions of Help Manuals* (included with the product or as part of the software)
- *Packaging materials* (box art, labels, inserts, envelopes, etc.)
- And more!

All of this is to say that today's translation and localization projects can be complicated and contain many "moving parts" that need to interact precisely in order to work. Fortunately, the best vendors will follow a proven and effective process to manage all of these components in a way that yields consistent, high quality deliverables. Of course, a good process also eliminates waste and inefficiency, thereby lowering costs.

It Starts and Ends with Project Management

Solid project management techniques are required to tie together different stages of production and make sure that all parties involved are cooperating as efficiently as possible. It should come as no surprise then that good communication is just as critical to a successful localization project as it is in any other field. A localization project manager (PM) should serve as the main communication conduit throughout the project's lifecycle. He or she is responsible for accurately relaying your needs and concerns to the rest of the project team, and vice versa.

These channels of communication must be open from the very beginning of any project. Typically, a primary client contact is identified to serve as the PM's counterpart. This person ideally has the authority to approve and/or delegate tasks. An additional point of contact on the client side might be an in-country resource who resides in the target country. This person can offer important input on terminology, style, and local technical issues, and can also perform quality reviews.

Together, the PM and the designated client contact(s) should review project details, including expected delivery format(s), at the beginning of the project. Once it is clear that everyone is on the same page, the PM should be able to confirm a delivery date consistent with the timeline developed during estimation. Discussing these items early is the best way to make sure your expectations are met.

Aaron Carlson

In traveling around and meeting with clients in the legal services and health care industries, it's evident that clear and concise communication is paramount. Our services help companies in communicating clearly (in over 200 languages!) with their customers and help patients attain better care at hospitals and clinics. It's a service that makes a huge difference in patient's care and lives while helping our clients save time and money. I'm originally from Minnesota and can help translate the Minnesota dialect of English (have you seen the movie *Fargo*?) if necessary!

Remember, you know your business better than anyone else, so communicate as much information as possible to your localization vendor before your project starts. This includes anything that may be helpful for translators to better understand your product, such as existing glossaries, terminology lists, or product descriptions.

During the project, you can expect your localization PM to keep the exchange of information fluid and to provide clearly defined status reports and/or reporting analytics. Status reports might be as informal as an email, or as formal as a posted report on a web-based collaboration platform. Be sure to request summary reports that meet your specific needs. The largest vendors may also offer a translation management system (TMS) that allows clients to view the status of their projects 24/7. See Chapter 16 for a more in-depth discussion of TMS tools.

Once your project is underway, the PM is responsible for assembling the project team, coordinating all of their activities, monitoring progress, troubleshooting, and completing the project on time.

But what exactly are the tasks that a PM needs to coordinate? The steps typically performed when localizing fall within one of the following seven disciplines. Each is a unique specialization that is ideally performed by skilled professionals who are specifically trained in that area.

- *Translation*
- *Copyediting*
- *Proofreading*
- *Engineering*
- *Desktop Publishing (DTP)*
- *Quality Assurance (QA)*
- *In-Country Review (ICR)*

Because no two projects are the same, a true solutions-based approach to language services means adapting the process to meet the specific needs of every project.

Workflow

The number of people involved and the type of work done to your files is predicated on the type of materials being localized. A small marketing flyer translated into a single language might require a relatively small six-person team, but a large operator's manual translated into multiple languages will require a much larger and more complex team. Depending on the word count, timeline, and number of languages needed, your PM will assemble a team of translators, editors, and proofreaders accordingly. In addition to the linguists, there also may be a team of desktop publishers; one or more QA reviewers to inspect the work as it is done; and at least one localization engineer to process and prepare all the files for each step.

How Many Translation Steps Do I Need?

As discussed in Chapter 5, translation quality is a function of the skill of the linguists who perform the translations, and the number of "Quality Assurance" steps performed by your vendor.

To ensure the highest quality results, most localization projects should include three distinct linguistic steps. Within the industry, this is often referred to as a "3-step" process:

1. *Translation*
2. *Copyediting*
3. *Proofreading*

Translation constitutes the bulk of the work and is the process of converting the source language into the target language. The second step, copyediting, entails a side by side review of each sentence pair to make sure everything was translated accurately, and to polish or clarify any imprecise language. Finally, the proofreading step is intended to catch any lingering typos, if they exist. This step is ideally performed "in context," either after a formatting pass or an initial build. If possible, each of these steps should be performed by a single, but different, full-time professional translator to ensure the highest quality translation possible. Depending on the size of your project, completing a 3-step translation could be as short as a couple of days or as long as several months.

If all you need is to understand the basic meaning of some text as quickly as possible, you may be channeling your inner Confucius and wondering, "Why use a cannon to kill a mosquito?" In this case, one translation step is undoubtedly enough.

This question gets to the heart of an important distinction in the industry between localization and document translation. For less complex projects, a "3-step" translation may not be needed. But how do you decide when "2-steps," or even "1-step" is appropriate for your needs? An experienced LSP will be able to walk you through all of your options based on the nature of your project.

Producing "Native Quality" translations

When your translation vendor uses the "right" translators and follows the "right" process, you should end up with a "native quality" translation. But what exactly does this mean? In simplest terms, a native quality translation will appear to the reader as though it was written from scratch by a native speaker of the target language who lives in the target language country. The second part of this definition, where the translator is based, should not be underestimated. For example, a French translator who was born and educated in France but who has lived in the United States for the last 20 years may not be able to produce native quality content if he or she is no longer familiar with the latest cultural references in France. At times, even living in the target country may not be enough. At LanguageLine, we once received feedback from a customer who said that our English to German translation was excellent, but the translator clearly lived in Austria rather than Germany. We knew that the translator really lived in Germany, but after looking at map, realized his home was only a few miles from the Austrian border.

ASK AN EXPERT:

How will new technologies reshape the role of human translators?

Salvatore "Salvo" Giammarresi, PayPal Head of Content & Globalization

Like all knowledge-based workers, the role of human translators has been, and will continue to be, reshaped by technology, particularly for those working in the tech industry. While I expect new technologies will focus on automating and facilitating the repetitive and time-consuming mundane parts of translation (like looking up terms in a glossary, searching for concordances in a corpus or retrieving previously translated segments), my hope is that in the future they will be truly designed around the translator, ultimately increasing the velocity and quality of their work. I envision this will allow translators to primarily focus on the uniquely human ability to understand the subtle nuances of complex and ambiguous source language as it relates to all other elements of the end-to-end customer experience, and masterfully convey it in the target language.

So just what makes someone a professional translator or linguist? The most important criteria are:

- *Native fluency in the target language and a near-native understanding of the source language,*
- *Training in the localization process, translation methodology and technology,*
- *Certification(s) as proof of their skill sets,*
- *Expertise in one or several subject matters, and*
- *Ability to use translation tools.*

Obviously, knowing the source and target language is the bare minimum. But without the right training, that skill only goes so far. It is imperative that a linguist be able to use the latest tools and make informed decisions during translation. Other important factors are:

- *Access to extensive reference libraries,*
- *Excellent writing skills, including a grammatical mastery of the target language and knowledge of various written forms and styles, and*
- *An acute awareness of cultural differences and language subtleties.*

While developing the English language source material, organizations typically use professional technical writers with subject matter knowledge. For precisely the same reasons, it also makes sense to hire professional linguists to translate these materials.

Your localization vendor should follow well-documented linguistic qualification procedures for evaluating and hiring individual linguists or translation agencies. In turn, the linguists they select from their team for your projects should be experienced and familiar with your content subject matter.

The Language Within a Language

To fully appreciate the skill that linguists must possess to produce great translations, it's helpful to look at a few examples that illustrate how a thorough understanding of both the source and target languages, as well as cultural and industry norms, is paramount. Localization involves much more than word-for-word "translation." Because different cultures use different grammar and sentence structures, straight word-for-word translations often do not reflect proper linguistic style or accurately capture complex ideas. Sometimes they no longer even convey the original meaning or message. An experienced linguist, however, will accurately translate the most difficult materials and will also convey nuances, ideas, and register (tone, style, formality, complexity, etc.).

Below are examples from several languages of how these aspects can be quite tricky. Fortunately, when it comes to localization, process is the key to success. So if you hire a localization vendor who has a good process, your project will be a success.

Process is the Key to Success

Spanish

Agreement on terminology
"Congratulations" can be translated correctly as Felicitaciones or Enhorabuena.

Local suitability
"Congratulations!" as well as "Welcome to … " are frequently used in user manuals to introduce a new product. Should the Spanish audience be addressed in this rather colloquial American way? Is there a more formal way to address the user, or should this greeting not be used at all?

Capitalization
One sign that you've mastered a language is that you know when to break the rules. By default, the Spanish language does not use title case, and only the first letter of a title would be capitalized.

e.g. *The guide to translation and localization* vs.
The Guide to Translation and Localization (title case).

Cedric Vézinet

There has never been a day in my 20 years in localization when I did not learn something, there is so much complexity to this industry beyond the translation itself. What is frightening is that I still remember everything I have ever learned! I could probably still move a Greek qsc from Windows 95 to MacOS 7.1 using a Netscape trick. A lot of useless information! This is probably the reason why I keep leaving my wallet behind everywhere I go … There is no more room up there!

A sign in a Chinese cafeteria

The Guide to Translation and Localization

Joseph Varda

For over 10 years, I have had the pleasure of helping many top F1000 and SMBs manage their global messaging needs. It is always exciting to be part of a company's growth as they expand their business into new international markets. Throughout the years, I have seen many changes in the translation, localization and interpreting industry. One thing I will tell you, with approximately 3.8 billion people in the world using the Internet to search for information, products, services, connections, etc. and for making purchases, your business needs to "speak their language" both written and verbally. Whether your company is looking to increase its market presence into more foreign countries or just starting out, LanguageLine is your "go-to-partner" and we will help you every step of the way.

For Spanish content that is intended for the US market, however, it has become commonplace to "Anglicize" the language, and many businesses want to retain elements of their English content, such as title case, in their Spanish translations even though it's technically "improper." The reasoning is usually that, for marketing pieces and other public facing documents in particular, they prefer that the content reflects where and how the content is being circulated. By doing so they achieve parity between all of their collateral, and even though the document is in a foreign language it doesn't seem foreign to the marketplace

Japanese

Depending on the platform, commands and buttons are translated differently:

Save As	名前を付けて保存	別名で保存
Print	印刷	プリント

Depending on the context, an English word can be translated into multiple terms in the target language:

Address	住所、アドレス
Title	題名、タイトル、役職
Class	クラス、級、階級
Time	時間、タイム

On the other hand, sometimes multiple terms in English can be translated into a single term in Japanese:

Tall	高い
High	高い
Expensive	高い
Pretentious	高い

Some words and abbreviations, by convention, stay in English:

lpi	lines per inch
pts	points
m/cm/mm	meter/centimeter/millimeter
g/kg/mg	gram/kilogram/milligram

German

Variation between software and hardware technology:

"Setup" is translated into "Einrichten" if the term refers to setting up the software, and "Anschließen" if the term refers to setting up a peripheral device.

Non-translated term

In projects where the documentation is translated but the user interface stays in English, the client and the localization vendor should decide whether the English term is followed by the localized term in parentheses OR the English term falls after the localized term.

Klicken Sie auf Load/Unload Panel (Stück laden/Entfernen), or

Klicken Sie auf Stück laden/Entfernen (Load/Unload Panel)

Style

"Connect your printer to the computer" can be translated formally into:

Schließen Sie den Drucker an den Computer an.

Or in the imperative voice:

Drucker an den Computer anschließen.

Or in the passive voice:

Der Drucker muss an den Computer angeschlossen werden.

ASK AN EXPERT:

What does language access mean now to your organization? In 5 years?

Laura Brandon, GALA Executive Director

Language is the unsung hero of globalization. We know that global business, global humanitarian efforts, global politics, and the spread of knowledge worldwide depend upon language and communication, even if it's the financial figures of globalization that often take center stage. GALA member companies enable language access, which is critical to the engines of commerce, information exchange, and public safety in so many sectors and scenarios. In 5 years' time, this work will be even more important as the global economy continues to grow, and people, products, and technology become more interconnected.

Chapter 7
Preparing Your Content for Localization

Creating your content with localization in mind can help you avoid frustrating delays and increased costs down the road as you expand into the global marketplace. Here are some tips to consider when developing your materials, whether it's a user interface (UI) for a software application, printed documentation, online documentation, multimedia content or a website.

Layout Issues: Allow for Text Expansion and Different Linguistic Features

As a general rule, assume that your English text will expand 20 to 30 percent when it is translated. It is vitally important that your document's layout leaves enough room (i.e., white space) for the target language. This cannot be overemphasized; formatting the translated document is far easier and more efficient when adequate space is available. Costs can rise dramatically when the translated text must be laboriously manipulated to fit within a cramped space. Never mind the fact that extra white space also makes your English version that much more readable.

Also, make sure your layout is designed in a way to accommodate the display of both LTR (left to right) and RTL (right to left) languages. If your layout mimics the orientation or other linguistic features of the English, some localized versions can appear unnatural or contrived.

For example, English is read from left to right, but Arabic and Hebrew are read from right to left. If you have background graphics like text boxes that lean to the right to reflect the reading order of English, Arabic and Hebrew versions will have to be heavily modified lest they look unprofessional or awkward. Similarly, if your layout results in the need for a lot of hyphenation, problems in other languages can arise. For example, German and Dutch have stricter rules for hyphenation than English, and line breaks might affect appearance.

Choose Graphics Wisely and Keep Text Editable

Visual messages may inspire very different meanings as they cross from culture to culture. For example, an image that is acceptable in Europe may be unacceptable in Asia or the Middle East. Use care here: A misstep might result in some embarrassment, but it also could detract significantly from your message and negatively impact your bottom line.

If possible, graphics should not contain text for the simple reason that it eliminates the need to translate it. If text must be associated with a graphic, try to create the text as a separate component in the page-layout application used to create the document (e.g., FrameMaker, QuarkXPress, InDesign). A callout or caption for a graphic should be a text block in the layout program. This requires less work to localize (saving you money), as the graphic text is part of the main document text and not a layer inside the graphic file. If you must include text in EPS graphic files, remember to leave it in text form. Do not outline the text, as this makes it very difficult and time-consuming to retype and translate.

Screen captures are a special category of graphics. By their very nature they often contain text. Translation of screen capture text is accomplished through localization of the software that was used to generate the English captures. Once the software is localized, the screen captures are regenerated. When creating the screen captures, be sure to generate all of them at the same screen resolution and scale, and then save the files in the same format used by the document layout application. You will also want to employ a logical naming convention that will help identify where they are placed.

Limit Your Font Types and Font Faces

When it comes to fonts, simpler is better. Try to keep the total number of fonts used in the document to a manageable number—no more than three or four, ideally, and select fonts that are available on both PC and Mac platforms. The fonts you do choose should be clean and crisply drawn, free of exceptionally thin serifs or wispy detail. Extra elements of detail in a font can make accents and special characters in foreign languages very hard to read, if they can be displayed at all.

The conventional combination of a standard serif font (e.g., Times) for body copy and a standard sans serif font (e.g., Helvetica) for headings is a good example of font selections that work well for translation. If custom or proprietary fonts must be used for branding purposes, expect to provide them to your localization provider. Not only will it reduce time and expense, but you will be sure to get the exact font you need.

Nhan Le

I go by Nan. Those who love me call me Nannie. I was born in Vietnam, grew up in beautiful Portland, Oregon and plan on many great years in Taiwan.

Reuse Your Content

Although you may earn style points for finding new and different ways to say the same thing every time a phrase or concept appears in your English source document, you're only increasing the cost of localization by doing so. Including lots of repetitions in the text will increase "leveraging percentages," which in turn lead to lower per word translation costs, and as an added benefit, will increase your reader's understanding of the content.

Single source content management systems are a great way to recycle your content not just within a single document, but across all output. If you're constantly reusing content that's already been translated, localization costs will be lowered. Make sure, though, that the templates and associated scripts you use for publishing take localization into account. Scripts that automatically capitalize titles, for example, rarely work correctly on translated content since capitalization rules vary by language. See Chapter 18 for more on this topic.

Moreover, a document that does not use style tags effectively (i.e., one that uses a different style tag each time to produce exactly the same formatting attributes) requires much more time to set up than a document that uses only one style tag to represent a uniform style. Using consistent style definitions throughout your document allows both PDF bookmark data and HTML style tags to be generated in localized files more easily.

Write Marketing Materials with Localization in Mind

Marketing materials may require special handling as they do not always localize easily. For example, the text and images that succinctly communicate your company or product to an American audience may not be relevant in Europe or Asia. We are all familiar with the stories about product names that take on a second meaning when introduced in another market.

ASK AN EXPERT:

Where do you see the language services industry in 5 years?

Florian Faes, Slator Co-Founder

As buoyant as ever. Demand for language services is essentially infinite. It is all a matter of price. Cloud-based workflows will be the norm (finally). Language service providers (LSPs) structured around email-based file project management will be vanishing as even conservative clients are embracing cloud-based solutions. Bring-your-own device remote interpretation will be much more common and accepted among both buyers and interpreters.

If possible, create your marketing materials with localization in mind, and keep the content as precise and globally understandable as possible. If this is not possible, be prepared to provide supplementary materials that will help explain the background, concept, and context behind your marketing campaign. At this point, localization may become less about straight-forward translation, and more about creating a message that evokes the same emotions and carries the same implications in the target language as it does in the source language while still maintaining its intent, style, tone and context. This service, which is called transcreation, is where your localization partner will prove their expertise and become invaluable to you.

Define Acronyms

Write out the full form of each acronym when it first appears in the source documentation. Later, when translated, the first use of the acronym should be both defined and translated in the target language, even if the acronym remains in its English form throughout the document.

Develop a Glossary as You Go

As you write, keep a separate list of terms that have special meanings. If you provide these terms and their definitions to your localization provider at the beginning of the project you will receive a much higher quality product at the end.

Error Message Management

All error messages that appear during installation, operation, or failure of a software application should be stored and maintained in a dedicated location. As new error conditions are exposed, any changes in verbiage between software versions or new messages should be added to the library with appropriate reconciliations from one version to the next.

Software Development—Specific Strings

Any branding or proprietary strings that appear within a user interface should be stored separately within the application. The goal is to collect a single worldwide source for these strings, with localized versions stored separately in language-specific folders or directories. Technical and data-centric strings that do not require translation should be kept with the primary source strings.

Concatenated Strings of Text

Special attention should be paid to concatenated strings of text (individual words linked together in a series or chain). For many reasons, it can be tempting to design your content, particularly your software UI, by using concatenated strings. Usually, these individual words and phrases would be stored in your database as discrete resources, but later combined in a specific order (according to your code) and displayed in your UI or published file. For example, when you work with only one language (English), it's + no + problem + to + create + the + rest + of + this + sentence + by + linking + individual + words + together + in + a + specific + order. If each of these pieces is a discrete resource, however, they would be submitted to your vendor and translated individually. The translator would not see the final product (the full sentence), but instead would be presented with a list of single words with no inherent connection to one another. The implicit assumption is that those translated pieces can then be recombined in the same way as the original English words to create a complete and accurate source in another language. The reality is that languages organize information differently according to their grammar and lexicon, and translations seldom have a direct, 1-to-1 correspondence. You cannot assume that each piece of your concatenated string will neatly correspond to a direct equivalent in a foreign language, or that those pieces would be strung together in the same order to create a complete sentence.

Style Guidelines

It is simply not possible to anticipate every issue you might encounter during localization. Even after taking great care to prepare and internationalize your material, you're still likely to run into situations where some sort of customization is required for a particular language. Style guidelines, or style sheets, that offer specific "rules" for the linguist to follow during the translation process are a good way to control the impact of unexpected issues. You may already have a corporate style guide for your source language, as well as for target languages you have previously localized. If not, your localization vendor can help you create them. Style guidelines typically address the following issues:

Desired tone (formal vs. conversational) of the localized documentation,

List of terms that should not be translated ("Do Not Translate" list),

Rules for capitalization, spelling of numbers, punctuation, and accent marks,

Translation of titles and subtitles,

Conversion of measurements,

List of dos and don'ts,

Acceptable font substitutes,

Guidelines for adjusting page flow,

Use of abbreviations, and

Cultural conventions, considerations, and *taboos.*

Style guidelines, developed in consensus with all stakeholders, help create high quality documents appropriate for the end user, for meeting company and country standards, and for maintaining geographic and cultural suitability.

> SE REALIZAN OBRAS DE RESTAURACIÓN, ROGAMOS EXCUSAS
>
> ---
>
> CONSTRUCTION'S WORK ARE TAKING PLACE THIS AREA, PLEASE, EXCUSE FOR THE MOLEST

A sign in Spain

CHAPTER 8
DTP: The Shapes of Language

For highly stylized documents, it is not enough to simply translate the words and let them fall where they may. Desktop publishing (DTP) professionals take great pride in recreating localized materials that have the same look and feel as the customer's source materials, while working around the characteristics of the target language. Not surprisingly, experience and access to the latest technology make a big difference in a vendor's ability to produce high quality deliverables. For example, Adobe Creative Suite and Microsoft Office 365 make it very easy to move content from one platform to another and, because they easily support Western, Asian, Cyrillic, and Semitic writing systems, are very localization friendly.

You can learn a lot about a language service provider's desktop publishing capabilities if you ask the right questions at the outset. Here are some things to consider:

Common DTP Questions From Localization Providers	
Font	Would you prefer to keep the same font sizes and allow the text to flow, increasing the page count?
	Or do you want to shrink the font to ensure that pagination, Table of Contents entries, and Index references match the English source document?
Leading	If you choose to shrink the font, should the line spacing (or leading) shrink proportionally?
Margins and Indentations	Can formatters "borrow" space from the margins?
	Can the indentations be shrunk to reduce white space to the left?
Headings	Can headings be made smaller? And, if so, should it affect all similar headings or only those that present a problem?
Justification	When long words expand to accomplish full justification, the spacing between the letters can stretch in ways that are uncomfortable to read. Can justification be turned off?
Hyphenation	Do you prefer to avoid hyphenation? In some languages this results in sudden line breaks.

Despite advances in technology, highly skilled DTP specialists are still vital to the success of most localization projects. Typically, vendors handle the desktop publishing in one of three ways. Some use their own employees, others outsource to DTP contractors (either off-shore or on-shore), and the rest leave it to the linguistic subcontractors who perform the translation work.

The differences can be significant, so do your homework. A skilled formatter knows many ways to ensure that your materials look as good in the new language as they did in the original. Also, with expertise comes efficiency. While the neophyte is searching for some way to squeeze text elegantly, the old pro simply reaches into a bag of trusted tricks. You shouldn't have to pay for someone else's on-the-job training.

Whether your vendor's DTP resources are located off-shore or on-shore can also affect your project. When timelines are critical or project complexity requires close coordination with other departments such as localization engineering or quality assurance (QA) testing, there are often significant advantages to keeping these tasks in-house.

Another key differentiator is the quality expectation that your vendor is trying to achieve. Some vendors ask their translators to format as they go, even if these resources lack professional training in this area. Others use DTP specialists, but only to perform a basic clean-up of the translated material.

The best way to ensure that you receive well-formatted deliverables is to ask for references and check them out. Also, ask the vendors if they outsource this important function or if they have their own DTP and QA departments. The vendors that are most concerned about providing high quality deliverables have their own internal DTP and QA departments.

Lastly, inquire as to how many years of experience the formatters have with the desktop publishing program you use. If the job requires a new program or a new version of a traditional program, make sure the vendor knows how to use it and that they have the appropriate target language version. Since the formatting for some languages can only be done on a native operating system, your vendor will need to have invested in a variety of systems and licensed publishing tools.

Even experienced formatters can get lost when working with other languages. Italicized Cyrillic or a Chinese document with multiple comma types can be downright confusing for the uninitiated. On the other hand, experienced localization formatters will already have dealt with most system, application, and file compatibility issues. If you are invited to visit the vendor's site, ask for a tour and a demonstration of capabilities.

Fonts

A well-chosen font can make a boring plain text document look exciting and dynamic, so it's no wonder then that many graphic designers use a wide variety of font styles and families. One of the most common challenges a DTP professional faces, though, is getting these fonts to cooperate with foreign languages. We've come a long way from the earliest dot pattern software fonts, but not all issues have disappeared. There are still many fonts out there that are not supported by Unicode, and some of the newest specialty fonts do not even support simple features like accented vowels or other diacritic marks. Obviously, this is a fundamental requirement for localized documents.

Depending on the font(s) used in your document, DTP professionals often have to select substitute fonts to get some text to display correctly in other languages. If you have selected the right vendor, there's no need to worry though. Experience and creativity go a long way in coming up with good solutions.

Another important point is that font issues are not always apparent to the untrained eye if you can't read the target language. In fact, what looks fine to a non-speaker may actually be garbled nonsense.

ASK AN EXPERT:

What do you think will be the next largest area of growth in this industry?

Jack Welde, Smartling Co-Founder & CEO

I think the next area of growth will be a mindset, rather than a method. The increasing availability of data-driven feedback will empower more companies to treat translation and localization as a profit center, rather than a cost center, and to expect predictable returns from their investments. Signals from a TMS and across the organization will confirm the positive business impact of localized content, letting executives know precisely which assets and which languages are justifying the associated translation expense. Those insights can then shape smarter strategies around what content should be translated, what workflows to apply for optimal returns, and which markets to develop.

What's worse, simply opening and closing a localized source file can corrupt a font if the wrong program is used or a particular font is unavailable on the system being used. Font corruption can also result in very subtle changes that are difficult to detect for even native speakers of the target language. This is especially true for languages that use characters or connecting script.

Text Expansion

When English is translated into other languages, it often takes more space to say the same thing. The reason may be that the new language uses more articles, as in French or Italian, or because the words are simply longer, as in Dutch or German. On the other hand, a few Chinese characters can express an entire phrase, resulting in text contraction. While text contraction is rarely a problem when localizing documents, text expansion can raise some tricky issues.

The standard rule of thumb in the localization industry is that European languages expand, on average, by about 30% (without hyphenation). This can cause several challenges. A table that fits on one page in English may spill over to the top of the next page in Greek. Similarly, section headings in large type might run to two lines. Indented text could leave large blocks of white space to the left.

At the beginning of the localization project, your translation provider should ask questions to determine how you want to handle text expansion. While these questions may be unfamiliar if this is your first localization project, with time you will become an expert, too.

By addressing these layout concerns at the beginning of the project, your localized documents will be much higher quality when they are delivered.

Online Documentation

Online documentation avoids some of the pitfalls of text expansion and page matching that are associated with printed materials, but it introduces engineering issues instead. For example, if your document is displayed on a computer screen in HTML or some other online format, expansion will not be a problem since the text will extend downward and the user simply scrolls down the page to read the "expanded" text. What can be an issue, however, is that your content may not display correctly on the operating systems and browsers available in your target market. By performing functional testing on native operating systems, your localization provider will be able to ensure that the applications perform and display as advertised. Be sure to discuss your specific engineering testing requirements with your vendor so that you are both clear on testing expectations.

Screen Captures

Almost all software documentation uses screen captures, which are no more than pictures or graphics of the software as displayed on screen, to tie together the references in the document to what the user sees on screen.

Just as translated text expands in the body of the document, translated dialog boxes may expand as well. One of the most common examples is an error message box. Due to text expansion, a screen capture of an error message that was originally 3 inches wide may expand to 3.5 inches after it's translated due to text expansion. If the new image is scaled back down to the size of the original, it could appear fuzzy or distorted when printed. Alternatively, the new image can be used at the larger size while the surrounding text is formatted to compensate. If your document uses screen captures, be prepared to talk with your localization vendor about how you would like these matters resolved.

Graphics

Working on the graphical assets of any source file can be difficult. In fact, when it comes to localization challenges, it doesn't get much worse than being asked to recreate localized versions of graphical elements without access to the source files (Photoshop, Illustrator, or CorelDraw, for example). This invariably requires additional time and budget for the DTP department, especially when gradient backgrounds and obscure fonts are used. To avoid these additional costs and delays, it is always a good idea to keep your source files in a safe place and to isolate localizable layers.

Another aspect to consider about page elements that contain text such as graphics and buttons is that they may need to be resized after translation. Similarly, online forms may require special engineering to support the user's ability to enter special characters, international phone numbers, and foreign addresses (along with any other special requirements requested by your international users).

Localizing Bidirectional Languages

Some languages are written right to left (RTL), but most applications, websites, and documentation are designed for languages that are written from left to right (LTR). This can create some interesting challenges when localizing into a RTL language. Fortunately, most formatting tools now have the ability to convert most documents from LTR or RTL if you know how to use them, but many adjustments will still be required.

Examples of RTL languages include Arabic, Hebrew, Yiddish, Farsi, and Urdu.

User Interface Layout

The direction of writing affects the way information should be presented and placed. For example, some applications use icons to tell users to go to the "Next" or "Previous" page. Because these icons do not have the same meaning when used with a RTL language, however, users often become confused.

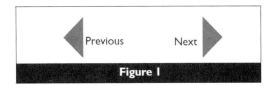
Figure 1

In Figure 1, the "Next" icon for the LTR language is correctly understood by the application. For the RTL language, however, the "Next" icon would be interpreted as "Previous." To fix this problem, the images need to be flipped horizontally (i.e., the one on the right is moved to the left and vice versa) and the underlying functionality must be changed as well.

Figure 2

Angelina White

Before joinging LanguageLine, I was a translator. One time, I remember being in a hurry to send out a batch of contracts. Later, I noticed some simple errors that I had not caught. Oops! After this, I meticulously reviewed all of my work to ensure it was perfect. Nowadays, I get to do this all day long for our linguists, and I have found that it's a lot more fun to find OTHER people's mistakes than my own!

RTL languages can also be confusing to users when following step-by-step instructions that are listed horizontally. The layout of a document may need to be modified for reading from right to left to ensure that the steps are followed in the proper order. Notice in Figure 3 how the following steps will be interpreted differently by users with different reading orientations:

Insert CD in CD-ROM drive	Install application	Click on the application's shortcut to start
Figure 3		

These steps can be easily completed if you read them from left to right, but if you translate them into a RTL language and leave them in the same order, the steps will be read from right to left and misinterpreted. The first thing the user will do is to look for the application's "Shortcut to start" without installing the application or even inserting the CD in the CD-ROM drive. Obviously, it is critical to modify the layout of the interface when localizing into a RTL language.

Combining Text from Languages with Opposite Writing Directions

When localizing into a RTL language, some information, like brand names, dates, addresses, and phone numbers does not get translated. A bidirectional document that has text with different writing directions forces the RTL text to be stored in reverse order around the LTR text. This makes the sentence meaningless and unreadable in most cases. Figure 4 contains a sentence that has a mix of Arabic and English words. Notice how the order of the words is misplaced in the text file and needs to be re-ordered to display correctly.

This is how the characters are stored in a text file.	في البحوثات الخاصة بي Google أنا استخدم موقع
This is how the characters should be displayed.	أنا استخدم موقع Google في البحوثات الخاصة بي
Figure 4	

In most text editors, you can choose the reading order to be right to left or left to right but this does not fix the issue entirely. It will only fix the reading order in that editor, but once the text is displayed in another application or device, the same problem remains.

One obvious way to get around this issue is to avoid using LTR text (such as English) in combination with RTL text (like Arabic). When mixing left to right and right to left text cannot be avoided, the order of the sentence will need to be reversed manually. This will allow you to upload your file to another application and display it correctly.

Alignment and Formatting

Your written content should be aligned to properly display and wrap text at the end of each sentence. If not, the order of the words and the meaning of the sentence will be incorrect. Fortunately, most applications have tools that can change the writing direction of the text. For example, markup languages like HTML have tags you can add to your code to adjust the "DIR attribute" and specify the base direction of text (LTR, RTL).

Most Middle Eastern countries use both Arabic and Hindi character sets for numbers (Figure 5). There is no consistent use amongst RTL language users and the choice of which digits to use is often determined by which character set the software supports.

Arabic Digits	0	1	2	3	4	5	6	7	8	9
Hindi Digits	٠	١	٢	٣	٤	٥	٦	٧	٨	٩

Figure 5

Whether you use Arabic or Hindi digits, numbers are written from left to right—with the most significant digits placed farthest to the left (Figure 6). Of course, this is the opposite of how the text is written in a RTL language.

European Digit	764
Arabic Digit	764
Hindi Digit	٧٦٤

Figure 6

Punctuation

Punctuation also can be a challenge in bidirectional localization. For example, the exclamation mark, period, and colon are displayed the same way in both Arabic and English while other punctuation elements, such as the question mark, comma, and semi-colon are reversed. In some text editors, when punctuation marks (that display the same) are added to the end of a sentence, they automatically move to the beginning of the sentence unless they are in the middle of a line (Figure 7).

Period at the end of the line is moved to the beginning.	.انا استخدم الحاسوب
Period between two sentences on the same line displays correctly.	انا استخدم الحاسوب. و ابحث

Figure 7

TEXT EXPANSION/CONTRACTION

Language	% difference
Arabic	104%
Chinese	61%
Czech	117%
Dutch	128%
English	100%
Esperanto	92%
Farsi	104%
Finnish	103%
French	111%
German	108%
Greek	128%
Hebrew	83%
Hindi	83%
Hungarian	113%
Italian	109%
Japanese	115%
Korean	123%
Portuguese	110%
Russian	115%
Spanish	117%
Swahili	88%
Swedish	95%

(George Sadek & Maxim Zhukov, Typographia Polyglotta, New York: ATypI / Cooper Union, 1997. The study compared the Preamble from the Universal Declaration of Human Rights in a variety of languages, with English as the base 100%.)

Chapter 9
How Do You Know If It's Any Good?

Perhaps you speak another language or even a few others. Still, chances are that you will not be able to personally check the translation quality for every project or language your organization commissions. Even if you had the linguistic skills, you probably don't have the time. So how can you be sure that you are getting the best translations possible?

The most effective option is to make sure your vendor has a comprehensive quality assurance (QA) program that is specifically designed to answer the following questions:

- Is the translation quality acceptable?
- Does the localized product look like the original?
- Does the localized product work like the original?

As you might imagine, the type and extent of quality assurance procedures performed has a direct impact on how good the translated deliverables you receive will be. Surprisingly, however, the QA reviews performed by many localization providers are minimal or non-existent.

In contrast, the best localization providers perform a wide range of quality assurance procedures on the linguistic, formatting, and functional elements of your project, as well as "regression checks" and other statistical measures to ensure the highest quality deliverables.

When considering possible vendors, be sure to ask about their QA methods. In an effort to cut costs or timelines, it can be tempting to only perform a cursory review or even skip this important step altogether. But once you consider all the hard work that went into creating your source content, you can see how investing in comprehensive QA is worth it.

It is always fascinating for those of us on the vendor side of the industry to see clients who spend weeks wordsmithing the English version of their website or documentation, and then several more weeks to ensure that the published versions are perfect, decide that they don't want to pay for or don't have the time to make the localized versions just as perfect. If the quality expectations of your customers are the same in all locales, a thorough QA process will help ensure that you meet the expectations of all your customers while protecting your localization investment.

Format QA ("Spot the Differences!")

At some point or another, you've probably seen a "spot the difference" game where two very similar images are placed side by side, and the objective is to find all the subtle differences. The visual review step in a localization process has a very similar objective.

This process can be customized, depending on the needs of the client and the purpose of the product.

If you are planning to localize marketing materials, high-end brochures, critical forms, technical publications, or any other customer-facing document that will be widely circulated, you will receive higher quality translations if you hire a vendor that employs quality assurance specialists to perform comprehensive Format QA of your deliverables. In simplest terms, these highly skilled professionals will perform a very thorough comparison of your source and target documents to make sure that everything, except of course the language, looks exactly the same.

Here are some examples of what QA specialists look for:

- No missing text,
- Nothing left in the source language,
- Consistent font type, style, and size,
- Correct text indentation and alignment,
- Thorough verification of numbers, timetables, currency amounts, etc.,
- Correct placement and size of graphics, as well as lines and callouts around them,
- If needed, matching of page flow and page numbering,
- Checking of cross-references between text and the table of contents, internal references, screen captures,
- Correct spelling of terms that remain in the source language, and
- Translation consistency for product or company names and other frequently used words/functions (such as "Close," "Next," "Edit," "File," etc.).

The better vendors likewise will know when exact matches are not appropriate. Sometimes certain information should appear differently in a localized document to reflect the target locale. Most of these adjustments will be identified in either the planning stage or during translation, but the QA review might also raise questions about how certain project-specific items should be handled. Typically, the LSP's project manager will reach out directly to you to answer these questions as they arise.

Some common non-linguistic and cultural elements that QA reviewers look for are:

- Units of measurement: Are the units of measurement used (inches/centimeters, pounds/grams, Celsius/Fahrenheit, etc.) appropriate for the target market?
- Correct local contact information for each language (phone numbers, addresses, e-mail addresses, website URLs, etc.).
- Date and time: Are the date and time format locally correct?

To help your vendor develop appropriate quality assurance guidelines for your project, be sure to provide them with any information that can aid the translation and QA steps early in the localization process. Some examples of helpful information are:

- Terms and names to remain in English,
- Terms that should appear in both English and the target language, and
- A list of part numbers for your product.

When a high quality product or high quality deliverables are paramount, your vendor can and should perform more than one regression check. After the first QA pass is completed and the requested changes are implemented, a second review can be performed to ensure that everything has been done as requested. Prior to delivery, the Project Manager should then perform one last review to ensure that every final change has been entered in the files correctly.

Michelle Williams

I was a language access coordinator in the health care sector for more than 10 years so you would think I could speak another language by now. Over this time I have learned so much; but just when you think you have seen it all something new comes along. When the inevitable happens and there is a zombie attack, having documents in multiple languages will definitely help people communicate and stay organized. If you are prepared for a zombie apocalypse then you are prepared for anything!

ASK AN EXPERT:
What does quality mean?

Toos Stoker, TAUS Digital Marketing Director

We have learned that assessing translation quality is the single biggest challenge in the translation industry. Most companies work with a static approach to translation quality. And when it comes to measuring that quality they fall back on counting linguistic errors. But linguistic errors do not always or rarely say much about tone, style, and other important quality factors. The increased usage of translation technology and the emergence of new dynamic content complicate the translation quality challenge even further. Buyers and providers of translation services need to be able to go up and down in quality. They need to deliver a dynamic service: a translation quality that matches the purpose of the communication. To help to facilitate this dynamic approach, we, together with our members, developed the Dynamic Quality Framework (DQF) in 2014 and harmonized it with the Multidimensional Quality Metrics (MQM) framework in 2015.

In other situations, however, a full-blown, multi-step QA process would be overkill. For example, if the translated materials are going to have a limited distribution, be for internal use only rather than client facing, or if you just need to know what something says, a different approach to QA should be taken. In these cases, the QA specialist will perform a comparison between the source and target document that focuses on accuracy and correct spelling of names, addresses, precise numbers and currency amounts, dates and times, and other relevant information. In other words, they only focus on what is critical.

Functional Testing

Just because everything looks right doesn't mean it works right. Functional testing makes sure the localized version of your product behaves the same way as the source you provided at the start of the project. Typically, this kind of testing is most important for software, but it is useful for anything with any kind of interactivity. Online and electronic documentation, for example, can also require functional testing to confirm that bookmarks, hyperlinks, and internal cross-references work as intended.

Typically, the files are checked for:

- Compatibility with native operating systems,
- Correct display of fonts and graphics using the native UI, or an appropriate browser or reader,
- Correct functioning of hyperlinks, bookmarks, fields, buttons, and
- Clear printing of pages.

This list may be customized with other items.

Software and Graphical User Interfaces (GUI)

To say software localization is a complex process is an understatement. In addition to performing all of the steps you would for any other localization project, you need to make sure you didn't break any of the oh-so-delicate components of the software in the process. Reviewing and exposing the relevant behavior of your localized software usually requires testing the resulting product on native operating systems. This is the best way to discover, document, and communicate issues that could compromise an application's integrity when it has been translated for a local market. Examples of some of the most basic issues to look for are:

- Character encoding and fonts are correct,
- Text expansion/wrapping does not result in truncated text strings,
- Conflicts with hot keys and keyboard shortcuts,
- Unicode or accented characters are accepted as input,
- Date and number formats are correct for the locale and not confusing, and
- Use of keys that actually appear on the local keyboard.

How Do You Know If It's Any Good?

Further testing should confirm that the localization process did not introduce any "bugs" into the software and that all areas of the software perform as intended. The level of testing should be customized depending on the specific needs of the project or specific requests from a client.

Testing localized software follows the same standards for regular software testing. Chances are that if you're localizing software, you and/or your development team are well aware of these details. Before beginning testing, it is recommended that you and your vendor review the nature of the product and consider the following:

- The extent and variety of localization and internationalization desired,
- Languages, regions, and character sets that are required for proper localization,
- Interfaces and files associated with the application, and
- The width and depth of testing coverage desired, in accordance with your time and budget constraints.

When all of these issues have been addressed to your satisfaction and a plan is developed, testing can start.

Thorough functional testing is important and should be conducted for all languages in all possible scenarios. You never know when error conditions might be unique to a particular localization of an application; for example, you might uncover a printing error that occurs only in a Spanish version of an application, or an installation error message that persists in all non-English versions.

Operations most frequently considered in functional testing include:

- Install, modify, and uninstall in different configurations (for example, a US English installation on a Dutch-localized machine).
- Menu functions and Hot Keys.
- Help links and file paths.
- Core application functions.
- Localized input device functionality (international keyboards, for example).
- Regional Default Settings: Do settings for items such as paper size, date/time, punctuation marks, and currency formats default to the appropriate settings for the country or region for which your machine is localized?
- Cutting, copying, and pasting special characters: Do they translate correctly on a localized system?
- Document transferability: Can saved documents created in the source version be used in the localized version?
- Compatibility with assistive technology for people who are impaired, such as magnification, screen readers, refreshable Braille displays, and speech recognition tools.
- Browser compatibility and function.

Bob Marone

My philosophy in sales has always been to be my client's champion, whether internally or externally, whatever it takes to help them achieve their project and individual goals or corporate mission. Now, having been a part of the language services industry for the last 5 years, my philosophy in sales remains the same but the work "feels" more important. By enabling companies to offer their products, services and solutions in any language, we not only help those organizations thrive, we often help people all over the world live a better life.

My philosophy on life is less profound. In the words of Herman Munster, "Life is real, Life is earnest, If you're cold, Turn up the furnace."

When Coca-Cola began looking for a suitable Chinese version of its name after launching the drink there in 1927, it found that some local shopkeepers had produced homemade signs using Chinese characters to replicate the sound of the words "Coca-Cola," without noticing that the characters in combination could be read as "female horse fastened with wax" or "bite the wax tadpole," according to Coca-Cola researchers. Coke tweaked the spelling in such a way as to take on an added meaning: "to permit the mouth to be able to rejoice."

Although the strings used in your software will likely have gone through a multi-step translation process, it is always a good idea to incorporate some sort of post-build linguistic check into your workflow. These efforts can be combined with other functional testing steps, or you can perform a separate online review (OLR). In the case of OLR, you and your vendor can prepare a script for a linguist to follow to review the translations in context and confirm the integrity of all linguistic elements.

Of course, regression testing may also be necessary to verify that defect fixes and modifications have worked. Has a previously reported error condition been corrected in the latest iteration of the software?

During and after testing, a "bug report" of all error conditions discovered during testing should be produced. Issues can be documented in a number of ways:

- Video,
- Screenshots,
- Electronic logs, and
- Hard copy logs.

Think High Quality from the Start

Methodical testing and review will ensure that a localized application can be released seamlessly into a target market. Don't, however, rely solely on these after-the-fact checks to preserve quality. Proper internationalization, including pseudo-localization testing, can identify or prevent many issues before significant efforts have been invested in formal localization. Hours spent here can save weeks later.

Likewise, you can apply the same principles to the production of all of your products, including documentation. In our experience, this important step is often overlooked during the planning phase of a project, resulting in timelines that don't allow for a thorough internationalization of the product or materials before starting development.

If you're not sure what you can do or don't have the resources to prepare your content for localization, your vendor can review and "clean up" your English documentation. A grammatically correct and consistent English document greatly facilitates the translation process. Similarly, consistent formatting style significantly improves the document localization process. Keep in mind that if you wait until after the translation process is completed, a poorly formatted paragraph will require fixing in each language. If you review and clean up the document before translation begins, the poorly formatted paragraph only needs to be fixed once!

Thinking about your need for quality assurance and other document localization issues early in the process will dramatically improve your final product. The more thought you put into preparing your products for localization, the more likely you will be to achieve higher quality, lower costs, and shorter timelines.

In-Country Review (ICR)

The ICR step is a final, collaborative quality check between you and your vendor. It should not be thought of as a chance to play Gotcha!, but rather an opportunity to let your colleagues, business partners, or other stakeholders in the target market review the localized files and provide specialized feedback to your vendor.

An ICR accomplishes several things: prior to release, it puts the files in front of an industry expert with first-hand knowledge of the material; it creates an opportunity to gain buy-in from your international partners; and it can increase your confidence in the quality of your vendor's work. Ideally, the reviewer(s) you designate for ICR were involved in or briefed on any preliminary efforts to develop glossaries or terminology lists. They should have the same information you gave your vendor at the start of the project so that stylistic differences at this late stage do not result in costly revisions.

ICR can add value to any localization project. The feedback received, both positive and negative, helps your vendor improve the quality of future deliverables. You should feel comfortable offering a candid critique of areas where your vendor failed to meet your expectations and, of course, praise for tasks well done.

Stylistic Preferences vs. Translation Errors

It is not uncommon for translation vendors to receive a frantic call from their clients upon completion of ICR saying that the translation is "awful." At LanguageLine, we find that in the vast majority of cases the "errors" are not mistakes at all, but instead reflect the stylistic preferences of the reviewers. For example, they may prefer the tone to be more formal rather than conversational or one term over another (e.g., house vs. home; car vs. auto). In other cases, the proposed change would actually introduce a grammatical or linguistic error. It is also important to understand that most vendors will attempt to match the style of the source materials, so even though your in-country reviewers may not like a translation, it may faithfully reflect the style of the source materials.

So what do you do when your translation vendor insists that their translation is correct and your reviewers say it is wrong? The very nature of language makes identifying the "correct" translation a very difficult endeavor. After all, there are many grammatically correct ways to express the same idea within one language, so it follows that there may be several acceptable ways to say that same thing in another language.

Leah Carter

My 14 years at LanguageLine have served me well in the multilingual world we live in. In my day to day job, I can speak multiple dialects of Accounting, and I am always the company's first call when we need Invoiced Revenue translated to Deferred Revenue. If I'm traveling, I know I'll always be able to talk my way out of any unexpected accounting trouble I might run into. Also, as the mother of a college student and twin 12-year-old boys, I am fully fluent in Adolescent.

The Guide to Translation and Localization

Pamela Dillon

PM Pamela picked a peck of pickled peppers. A peck of pickled peppers, PM Pamela picked. If Pamela picked a peck of pickled peppers … she procured a plant someplace that pre-pickles peppers and should purvey a prodigious, preternatural pepper pursuit! Perhaps? Please! Poetic Pamela passionately passes on pepper profits— preferring professions pertaining to polishing prose, pretentiously precluding plebian produce pastimes. Puh!

Setting aside preferences, however, it is possible to reach a consensus as to whether two grammatically correct expressions in two languages convey the same information. The best ways to do this are:

- An independent, bilingual resource compares the translation with the source and provides her or his judgment;
- An independent resource "backtranslates" the translation in question into the source language and you compare that result to the original source; or
- A tester reviews the target language without any knowledge that it is a translation and summarizes the meaning. If the tester can glean all relevant information from the translation, that is the sign of a good translation. For example, if the source content contains instructions, you can see if the reviewer is able to follow them reading only the target language.

Resolving ICR feedback should be a collaborative process between your vendor and your reviewers. Professional translators have no pride of authorship and will be willing to incorporate stylistic preferences if that is what you want (although some firms may charge extra if the changes are extensive). On the other hand, actual translation errors will always be fixed at the vendor's cost.

Conclusion

When selecting a localization vendor, look for a partner that cares as much about your materials as you do. A good way to determine this is to inquire about their QA procedures. There are many translators and translation companies in the marketplace, but each one has different quality standards for their work. In the end, however, it's pretty simple. The only way to be certain that your translations are as good as you want them to be is to find a vendor who performs enough QA to ensure that they are!

**YOU ARE MY LOVE MY ANGLE
DON'T TREAT ME LIKE POTATO
我当你如珠如宝，你当我咸鱼水草**

A souvenir from China

CHAPTER 10
Getting the Language Right

There is a saying that the difference between a language and a dialect is the size of the army. Winston Churchill famously remarked that the US and the UK are two countries separated by a common language. The point here is that in many cases a language and a dialect share nearly identical vocabulary, and the differences between them are shaped more by geographical, cultural and political boundaries than linguistic ones.

For example, a Dane, a Swede, and a Norwegian can speak their own "language" at a party and for the most part understand each other. On the other hand, the variation among the German dialects is so considerable that only neighboring dialects may be mutually intelligible. Low German, most Upper German, High Franconian dialects, and even some Central German dialects when spoken in their purest form, are not intelligible to people who know only Standard German.

When selling to consumers abroad, it is critical to understand these linguistic nuances. Rather than focusing on languages and dialects, however, we believe it is more useful to think of different language varieties as "locales," and then to identify in which locales your target audience is located. Choosing the right locales will maximize the return on your localization investment, even if it means producing two versions for the same language. Below we discuss some of the more common languages where these very important distinctions arise, namely French, Spanish, Portuguese, and Chinese.

شاطئ رملي صالح للسباحة

Sand beach useful for swimming

سوئمنگ کے لئے مناسب ایک سینڈی ساحل سمندر

A sign in the United Arab Emirates

The Guide to Translation and Localization

Yasha Poursafar

I'm proud to be part of LanguageLine Solutions and work side by side with some very intelligent and strong people. We all bring something unique and valuable to the team, helping it grow more and more towards advancement, and I'm the little Persian girl who's very dedicated and happy to be part of the team.

Spanish (Iberian vs. Latin)

Spanish localization represents one of the most obvious opportunities to expand the market for your products. Approximately 470 million people living in more than 20 countries worldwide are native Spanish speakers. In the United States alone, there are 41 million native speakers plus a further 11.6 million who are bilingual. This puts the US ahead of Colombia (48 million) and Spain (46 million) and second only to Mexico (121 million) in the total number of Spanish speakers. Furthermore, the US Census Office estimates that the US will have 138 million Spanish speakers by 2050, making it the biggest Spanish-speaking nation on Earth, with almost a third of its citizens speaking Spanish as their first language.

The popularity of Spanish creates an interesting challenge for localization because the language has evolved differently in each region of the world. Most language service vendors offer two basic flavors of Spanish: Iberian Spanish, which is the Spanish spoken in Spain, and Latin American Spanish, which generally refers to Spanish that would be familiar in Argentina, Colombia, Mexico, Cuba, and Puerto Rico (to name few countries), and even the United States. But this split is also an oversimplification as there are clear linguistic variations and peculiarities that characterize the Spanish used in each locale. Of course, there are also practical elements that come into play when deciding in to which versions to localize. For most companies it would be cost prohibitive to pay for a Cuban version and a Mexican version, especially because Cubans and Mexicans alike would most likely understand the same "Latin American" Spanish.

Most global companies conclude that Iberian and Latin Spanish are sufficiently different to justify translating into both. Still, some companies prefer to have only one Spanish version, so they opt for a compromise that is known in the industry as *International* Spanish. *International* Spanish is rendered in a way that removes the distinguishing features that give locales a particular "flavor." The result is a "neutralized" form of the language that is not suitable for marketing materials and other related content. But is does keep the accountants happy because you only pay for one version!

Likewise, most language service providers also offer what is known as *US Spanish*. This version is frequently requested by organizations that need to support the 53 million Spanish speakers in the US (e.g., banks, insurance companies, health care organizations, and government agencies at all levels). US Spanish is also generalized to reflect the reality that its target audience is a composed of speakers from many different countries and backgrounds, but its most defining characteristic is that it targets people who are living and working in a mostly-English speaking country, and, whether they speak English or not, must navigate a bilingual world.

The differences between all of these varieties of Spanish can be quite subtle. Generally, they obey the same grammatical and spelling rules. A well-educated native speaker in any locale can read content produced in any other country. Subtle, however, does not mean insignificant, and there are important differences in vocabulary to consider.

For example, the words used for "potato" and "juice" are different in Mexico ("papa"and "jugo") and Spain ("patata" and "zumo"); and the word for "peanut" in Mexico is "cacahuate," but "maní" in most other countries in

South and Central America. Another important example of a difference in vocabulary, which in this case is a direct consequence of geography, is the word used for "computer." In most Latin American countries "computer" is rendered as "computadora." Spaniards call a "computer" an "ordenador" from the French word "ordinateur." Also, there are cases where the same word means very different things in different places, and the consequences can be significant. A commonly used verb in Spain meaning "catch," "grab," or "grasp," refers to something else entirely in Mexico and is considered vulgar and offensive.

In the United States, the situation is even more complicated as Spanish speakers have emigrated from many different countries and brought their regional language quirks with them. This diversity and the influence of English have even resulted in the emergence of a neutral accent often heard on the radio and on TV but not associated with any particular region or country. Written Spanish in the US, too, has its own idiosyncrasies that allow for and mimic features of the English language.

Locale can influence other non-linguistic factors as well. The decimal and thousand separators are good examples. Mexico and Central America use these separators in the same way as the United States (where one thousand twenty is represented 1,020.00). South American countries prefer the European way of expressing separators (where one thousand twenty is represented 1.020,00).

Given the complexities of the Spanish picture, how do you know which locale is right for you? At a minimum, you must decide between Iberian and Latin Spanish. If you are trying to reach a general, worldwide Spanish-speaking audience, doing both will *probably* cover your bases. Alternatively, if you must reach a very specific audience, such as affluent Spanish-speaking consumers in Colombia, your localization partner should have an experienced and diverse team of linguists who can provide that expertise. Knowing your target audience will allow you to select the right locale to best reach them.

ASK AN EXPERT:

What does language access mean now to your organization? In 5 years?

Dr. Nitish Singh (Ph.D. MBA, MA), Brand2Global Program Leader (Global Digital Marketing & Localization Certification)

I think for many organizations language access is determined by their market reach and target consumers. However, more companies are realizing they need to not only translate in major local languages but also local dialects. Take for example English usage in the UK and USA, and imagine using the same dictionary for the database for both countries. I am sure your British end users will be very frustrated when they are searching for Jumper or Trainers. So 5 years from now I think companies will pay more attention to local dialects and regional languages. Take for example the Indian market wherein you have about 22 official languages spoken by millions of people.

A sign at a bus station in Costa Rica

Portuguese (Portugal vs. Brazil)

Eric Manning

"Solutions Architect." Cool title. What's cooler is that it means I get to spend my days solving problems. What kinds of problems, you ask? ALL kinds—but it comes down to anything that gets in the way of our team providing you translations that are better, faster, and cheaper. It's an exciting challenge, and it's different every day.

Nearly 260 million people speak Portuguese throughout the world. Like Spanish, Portuguese is not homogeneous. Its forms differ in grammar, spelling, pronunciation, and vocabulary, especially between the two largest locales: Portugal and Brazil. A neutral or international form of the language is even less tenable than with Spanish, despite the fact that the Portuguese and Brazilians can understand each other. The differences are significant enough that it is very rare for companies to translate their materials into one type of Portuguese for both markets.

Brazilian Portuguese was not only influenced by native languages such as Tupinambá, spoken by the indigenous people of the Amazon, but also by the many languages spoken by African slaves. Although some Brazilian words made their way to Europe, most were only used in Brazil. Later, Southern Brazil absorbed a large influx of immigrants of Italian, German, and Japanese descent. These groups also influenced Brazilian Portuguese. European Portuguese, meanwhile, was influenced by the French spoken during Napoleon's occupation of Portugal.

In the 20th century, the linguistic split between European and Brazilian Portuguese widened as the result of technological innovations that required new vocabulary. Lately, Brazilian Portuguese has also been influenced by North American culture. For instance, Brazilian Portuguese translates the word "user" as "usuário" (a word that does not exist in European Portuguese dictionaries). European Portuguese translates "user" as "utilizador," similar to the French "utilisateur."

Internet World Magazine published a list in their Brazilian edition that pointed out some additional differences:

English	Brazilian Portuguese	European Portuguese
to access	acessar	aceder
mouse	mouse	rato
screen	tela	ecrã

Besides words that are completely different and/or used in a completely different context between these two variants of Portuguese, there are approximately 400 words with a different spelling and 1,500 with a different accent mark. Toss in some grammatical differences, and it's easy to see why many global corporations pay for translations in both versions of the language when entering both locales.

When localizing into Portuguese, be aware of these differences. Your localization provider should distinguish between European and Brazilian Portuguese and should use native speakers from the appropriate country to localize your product. Although Portuguese speakers from both sides of the Atlantic usually can understand each other, not localizing separately for each market can lead to confusion among your end users.

French (France vs. Canada)

There are now nearly ten million French speakers in Canada, mostly located in the province of Quebec. Over the past 400 years, the French spoken in this region has evolved dramatically, due in large part to its distance from French speakers in Europe and its close proximity to English speakers in Canada and the United States.

Canada has certainly become a prime target market for localized products. In 1988, the Canadian government passed the Official Languages Act, which conferred equal "official language" status to both English and French. This was done in order to preserve the nation's French linguistic heritage and to "support the development of English and French linguistic minority communities and generally advance the equality of status and use of the English and French languages within Canadian society." As a result, all official federal government communications must be issued in both languages, and government services must be available in both languages. Many commercial products follow the government's lead and provide packaging, labeling, and so forth in both English and French.

However, if you provide European French to a Canadian audience, you may be missing the mark. Canadian and European French differ in many ways, including vocabulary. Some differences include the following:

English	Canadian French	European French
telephone handset	le récepteur	le combiné
You're welcome.	Bienvenue	De rien (and several others)
blueberry	le bleuet	la myrtille
soccer	le soccer	le football
snowbank	le banc de neige	la congère
go shopping	magasiner	faire des courses

In addition, there are differences in pronunciation, in pronouns, in verbs, and in usage.

What, then, should you know when deciding whether to translate into one or the other or into both? French Canadians understand any material translated in European French because the written languages are generally similar, the differences listed above notwithstanding. Unlike Portuguese and more so than Spanish, though, the European variety can serve as a viable international version, appropriate even for certain African locales. The expense of translating into multiple locales for French may be unnecessary.

There may still be considerable benefits to picking a specific locale, however. If you want your target audience to feel that your product has been custom-made for them and avoid cultural sensitivity issues, you should translate content into a specific locale. This can usually be accomplished by having the work of a French translator copyedited by a colleague from the target country.

Carrie Lyn

Carrie Lyn is an avid motorcycle rider and multimedia expert who specializes in localizing training courses, videos, and other interacitve content. She loves riding her Harley to work each morning to help create a more connected global community where people communicate and share ideas despite differences in languages and culture.

Chinese (Mandarin vs. Cantonese, Traditional vs. Simplified)

Chinese far and away presents the most complications when considering the appropriate locale for localization. Where your translations will be used will dictate very important decisions about which spoken dialect is appropriate and which writing system should be used.

First of all, spoken Chinese consists of dozens of different dialects, often mutually unintelligible from one another. Pu Tong Hua, known as "Mandarin" in most Western countries, and Cantonese are the two most widely spoken Chinese dialects. As early as the second century BC, during the Han dynasty, language reforms were implemented in an attempt to standardize the language. Mandarin evolved from the language used by Chinese government officials and scholars centuries ago and to this day, is the "official" Chinese spoken language in the northern region of China. Taiwan and Singapore also use Mandarin as their official language. Cantonese, on the other hand, is a dialect widely spoken in the southern regions of China, such as the Guangzhou and Hong Kong areas.

Mandarin and Cantonese are the most widely spoken Chinese dialects, but they are by no means the only ones. For day-to-day conversation, many people prefer to speak in the dialect of their respective regions. Often two people speaking two different dialects cannot communicate verbally. They can, however, communicate in writing because of the standardization of the Traditional and Simplified writing systems.

The origin of the Chinese writing system is pictorial, dating back thousands of years. People drew pictures to express their thoughts—in short, to communicate. As you can imagine, this method of written communication was very cumbersome, making complex thoughts difficult to express. As a result, a number of reforms have been initiated to stylize and simplify the manner of writing Chinese. This has, in turn, resulted in a more uniform writing style.

Of all the language reforms initiated over the past two millennia, none has had a greater impact than the one carried out by the People's Republic of China (PRC) after its establishment in 1949. The mid-20th century language reform simplified the characters used in the Traditional Chinese writing system by reducing the number of strokes needed to write a character. The end result was the Simplified Chinese writing system. The PRC and Singapore currently use the Simplified Chinese writing system, while Hong Kong and Taiwan use the Traditional Chinese writing system. However, now that Hong Kong has been integrated into the PRC, we may see an increase in the use of Simplified Chinese there.

It is generally easier for a person who knows Traditional Chinese to understand Simplified Chinese characters than a person who knows Simplified Chinese to understand Traditional Chinese characters. However, this is not a sure thing. Moreover, using one of the standard writing systems is still not always sufficient for proper localization. For example, the Traditional Chinese used in Taiwan is somewhat different from that used in Hong Kong. The character set is the same, but they are sometimes grouped differently to express various concepts. One example of this is the term "lunchbox." In Hong Kong, this term is expressed by pairing the character for "rice" with the character for "box," while in Taiwan they use a pair of characters that roughly translate as "convenience now." A Hong Kong reader unaware of Taiwanese culture would understand the characters but not grasp the lunchbox connotation. If you are planning to localize for the Hong Kong market or for the Singapore market, you should plan a special copyediting step to customize your translations for those specific markets.

Continuous efforts at language reform introduced the use of the Roman alphabet to "spell" the pronunciation of Chinese characters. The result was the standard Pin Yin spelling system that is widely used in China, Taiwan, and Singapore today.

So, what is Chinese? You can see now that it really is a "blanket term" for several major dialects and two major writing systems.

Country	Spoken Language	Written Language
PRC	Mandarin	Simplified Chinese
PRC Guangzhou Province	Cantonese	Simplified Chinese
PRC Hong Kong	Cantonese	Traditional Chinese
Singapore	Mandarin	Simplified Chinese
Taiwan	Mandarin	Traditional Chinese

The next time you hear someone say, "We need this translated into Chinese," you should first think about what the term "Chinese" really means!

Many of the examples of language variation discussed above, such as different accents and different words for the same thing, may seem relatively benign. While that is sometimes the case, they are still dead giveaways of an intended locale. Ignoring them may defeat the purpose of localization, which we defined earlier as the process of adapting content to various markets or localities so that it seems natural to that particular region. For multimedia content with voiceover especially, it would be ill-advised to disregard these differences. If you produce your content first for one market and then try to reuse it in another country, you risk offending and alienating your target audience as it can leave the impression that they are an afterthought.

ASK AN EXPERT:

How will new technologies reshape the role of human translators?

Toos Stoker, TAUS Digital Marketing Director

The time machines will outshine human translators in transforming a text from one language into another is nearing. The moment that happens is referred to as the singularity. The debate is out there whether this singularity is something we should really wish for. The idea of it could easily lead to depressing and devastating visions of our industry's future and, as a result, put us in a defensive and reactive or inactive state of mind. The fact is that we are so far ahead on this track, it has become hard, if not impossible, to reverse the course. What we must do is be realistic about it and have an open mind about both the upsides and the downsides.

CHAPTER 11

It's the Law: Complying with Language Access Mandates at the State and Local Government Level

In the United States we use the term limited English proficient (LEP) to describe someone whose first language is not English or someone who struggles to read, write or understand English. Recent US Census data shows there are a record 63.2 million US residents who speak a language other than English at home (see chart below). That's one out of five people! This same data also says that this LEP population speaks 380 different languages, but a closer look at the survey shows that there is actually an even larger array of unique dialects. As we saw in the previous chapter, "speaking Chinese" can mean a lot of different things.

Top 10 Languages by Population

	Language	Count
1	Spanish	39,254,342
2	Chinese	3,139,432
3	Tagalog	1,688,494
4	Vietnamese	1,458,173
5	French	1,219,825
6	Korean	1,131,339
7	Arabic	1,117,304
8	German	934,438
9	Russian	890,120
10	French Creole	795,521

Source: 2014 American Community Survey, US Census, Language Spoken at Home

Immigrants are having an amazing impact on our economy. Consider this: Immigrants founded 18% of the largest companies in the US. And a report issued by the Partnership for a New American Economy found that immigrants were 60 percent more likely than native-born citizens to start their own businesses, which creates new jobs for everyone. Also, according to a report entitled *The Economic Benefits of Immigration*

It's the Law

by the Center for Latin American Studies at the University of California, Berkeley, because immigrants are more willing to move for work than native US citizens, this population "helps slow wage decline in stagnant regions and contributes to economic growth in booming ones." In other words, cities grow and small towns are rejuvenated where immigrants settle.

Language data from: cms.gov
Map courtesy of the Cartographic Research Lab, University of Alabama

Without a comprehensive language access strategy, government agencies might miss a large portion of these immigrants when they need to communicate about issues such as health, safety and social programs, or any other important message. To address this situation, many federal, state, and local government agencies have instituted language access mandates; and yet, too often, LEP people in the US still lack access to the information they need in the language they speak.

Title VI of the Civil Rights Act of 1964, 42 U.S.C. 2000d, et seq. and its implementing regulations provide that no person shall be subjected to discrimination on the basis of race, color, or national origin under any program or activity that receives federal financial assistance. Language can be a barrier for LEP individuals when accessing important benefits or services, understanding and exercising important legal rights, and reading information from federally-funded programs and activities.

Jon Bove

Jon Bove has been in the language access industry since 1995. His mission has been to assist government and industry organizations improve their outreach to limited English proficient constituents and customers here and around the world. Of particular interest is helping customers simplify and improve their English source content before translation, which improves readability and saves money.

Lani Chu

I love food. If I could do anything in the world, I would eat every minute of the day. Unfortunately, my limited foreign language skills only allow me to order dim sum at Chinese restaurants and sushi at Japanese restaurants. So I asked myself, where is the best place to expand my culinary vocabulary? With the hope that I would soon be able to order any type of food from any country, I stepped into the world of localization and expanded both my gastronomic and cultural horizons.

From Labor.NY.gov: "In New York State in 2011, Governor Cuomo issued Executive Order 26, which directed state agencies to provide language assistance services (translation and interpretation) to people of Limited English Proficiency. Agencies are required to prepare a Language Access Plan that identifies the most widely used languages by LEP individuals who access their services. Vital documents shall then be translated into these specific languages."

The U.S. Department of Justice Language Access Assistance Guide states, "vital written documents include, but are not limited to:

- consent and complaint forms;
- intake and application forms with the potential for important consequences;
- written notices of rights;
- notices of denials, losses, or decreases in benefits or services;
- notices of disciplinary action;
- signs; and
- notices advising LEP individuals of free language assistance services."

Non-compliance with language access regulations may affect funding. The Federal Inter-Agency Website, LEP.gov, states:

> "All recipients of federal funds and all federal agencies are required by law to take reasonable steps to provide meaningful access to limited English proficient persons. This means that, even if recipients operate in jurisdictions in which English has been declared the official language under state or local law, these recipients continue to be subject to federal nondiscrimination requirements, including those applicable to the provision of federally assisted services to persons with limited English proficiency.

> All recipients should be aware that despite the State's or local jurisdiction's official English law, Title VI and the Title VI regulations apply. Thus, recipients must provide meaningful access for LEP persons. State and local laws may provide additional obligations to serve LEP individuals, but cannot compel recipients of federal financial assistance to violate Title VI.

> For instance, given our constitutional structure, state or local 'English-only' or official English laws do not relieve an entity that receives federal funding from its responsibilities under federal nondiscrimination laws. Entities in states and localities with 'English-only' or official English laws are certainly not required to accept federal funding—but if they do, they have to comply with Title VI, including its prohibition against national origin discrimination by recipients of federal assistance. Failing to make federally assisted programs and activities accessible to individuals who are LEP may violate Title VI and the Title VI regulations."

Based on the information above, it is clear that localizing content for just one or two languages might constitute a failure in adherence to law, and result in penalties as well. So providing in-language access services under Title VI and numerous state and local executive orders is not just the law: It's a good thing. Getting this good thing done, however, is easier said than done.

Obstacles to Language Access Programming: Training, Champions, Psychology

A successful language access program is not just about funding, although that's always a major factor of course! Frequently, there is a lack of internal support for language access within the government agencies themselves. Promoting language access programs benefits everyone. Once these programs are in place and the staff becomes accustomed to working with translation vendors, even those who were reluctant to use translation services cannot imagine their lives and workplaces without a language access program in place.

Another common hurdle is insufficient employee training. English speaking government managers and their reports should be trained how to order translations, as well as **when**, **where** and especially **why** to do so.

The last major impediment is perspective. Those who are reluctant to use translation services need to cross a "bridge of understanding." There has to be a shift in mindset to recognize that translation is not "strange" or "complicated," but rather a logical and immensely practical solution for communicating across cultures.

Think about it this way. If constituents cannot read letters and notices issued by their local government, they might miss out on a lot of important information. For example, across the US, public signage in foreign languages keep immigrants (and tourists!) informed. Here are some other examples of popular translation requests from government agencies:

- Translated signage for public hospitals, public transportation, emergency services, and educational programs;
- Public assistance forms (Medicaid, Medicare, food stamps, low-income housing assistance);
- Insurance enrollment forms and announcements;
- Public health announcements and press releases regarding current outbreaks and initiatives targeting preventive measures;
- Applications and instructions for business licenses and renewals;
- Workplace notices, complaints, and regulations; and
- Student registration forms, enrollment guides, parent letters, health forms, transportation forms, free or reduced fee meal forms, field trip permission slips, and other K-12 public school- related outreach.

It's the Law

ASK AN EXPERT: How will new technologies reshape the role of human translators?

Winnie Heh, Career Advisor for Translation, Interpretation, and Localization Management at Middlebury Institute of International Studies at Monterey

When I was studying for my M.A. degree in Translation and Interpretation in the late 80's, the word "localization" did not even exist and there was no such thing as CAT tools. Fast forward 25 years, localization has enabled organizations, public and private, to expand their reach and thus increases the demand for language expertise. Various CAT tools have increased the through put of translators. When the issues of new language technologies come up, a commonly asked question is: "At what point will human translators be replaced?" I don't see replacement as a possibility, but redefinition of their role has happened and will continue to evolve.

(continued on next page)

The Guide to Translation and Localization

ASK AN EXPERT:

How will new technologies reshape the role of human translators?

Winnie Heh, Career Advisor for Translation, Interpretation, and Localization Management at Middlebury Institute of International Studies at Monterey (cont.)

I see three key ways of how technology defines human translators:

1. Translators need to have an insatiable appetite for the beauty of the languages as well as evolving technology.
2. Translators need to focus on per-word rates as well as increased earnings through speed and efficiency.
3. New positions have and will continue to be created in the language industry. This opens up a world of career opportunities for language professionals. Those who are willing and able to acquire new expertise and knowledge will have unprecedented levels of professional mobility.

Choosing a Vendor

The ideal translation vendor for government agencies will have experience working with local, state and federal organizations in the US, and they should take the work seriously. Thousands, if not millions (in some locales), will be impacted by the quality of the translated deliverables.

When choosing an LSP, you also will want to identify your key stakeholders. These might be administrators, lawyers, writers, or communications departments. By assembling a team that's committed to the success of your language access program, and then defining requirements and setting expectations with your vendor from the outset, you will be able to forge a successful collaboration.

Lastly, when selecting a vendor, you will want to pick one with a training or implementation team to help launch the language access program. Some vendors can even offer free coaching for writing better content before translation, again saving you money and making your message clear.

"Simple English"

Because most vendors charge based on the number of words translated, using "plain" or "simple" English will reduce translation cost and shorten the time needed to complete projects. Perhaps equally important, it also makes your outreach easier to understand ... and therefore more effective. Or, as one might say if they "simplified" it: Simple English makes simple Spanish.

In our experience, "plain English" or "simple English" is a concept that everybody talks about, but few actually abide by. Good simple English usually requires only 30 to 40% of the number of words that are found in a typical document, which is a huge savings when you are paying by the word. If your users want faster, better, cheaper, the answer is easy: Make your writing simple and concise.

So what is the key takeaway here? With budgets tight and funding scarce, many government agencies focus on the price they pay per word to minimize cost. But all this does is lead to poorer translations. Real savings are achieved by (1) writing better, shorter English, (2) understanding what translation vendors do and how to work more closely with them, and (3) keeping multilingual content in mind when you create your English source documents.

Quality Matters: The Benefits of Hiring a Professional Translation Company

While it is tempting to have your own in-house employees translate your documents, as we explained earlier, just because someone speaks another language doesn't mean he'll be able to provide high quality translations. Most of the time, they're entirely unqualified to translate documents, and allowing them to do so could actually endanger immigrants and other LEPs. But even if you're fortunate enough to have someone on staff who is a talented translator, it is still just one translator. A good translation vendor will have a second translator, and often a third equally qualified translator review every translation to make certain it is correct. They will also have translation tools; professional formatters and quality assurance specialists; highly experienced project managers; and a large team of professionals that they can call on when time is of the essence to quickly and accurately complete your project.

So just because your budget is already squeezed and bilingual employees seem like a fantastic and knowledgeable resource, tread carefully.

Web Localization and Other Online Content

It's no secret printed material has given way to the digital era, and more and more content is now hosted online. You may be wondering what to do about language access for your online materials. One tactic has been to use the Google "translate this" button. As explained in Chapter 3 of this book, however, this form of automatic translation is likely not a viable solution for your needs. It may be suitable for getting the "gist" of what the original says, but it does not provide equal access to your LEP constituency.

Websites and online content can be more complex to translate than basic document translation. In fact, in most cases, localization vendors will need to employ highly skilled localization engineers to successfully complete these projects. But be forewarned: Many vendors do not have these resources.

There are additional considerations as well. These include (a) platform and file structure; (b) how the content is accessed and reviewed by translators, engineers and reviewers; (c) how builds will be done and who will do them; (d) managing subsequent updates to ensure that changes to your English content are reflected in your translated content in a timely fashion; and (e) government internet and intranet security restrictions. It is not uncommon for government agencies to restrict access to files and require translators to work on their servers for added security. These constraints can significantly affect the time and cost to complete your project. Consider discussing translation of your online applications and web content early in the process to avoid unnecessary delays and added cost.

Sometimes government agencies think that translating online information isn't "worth" the cost, especially if there is no apparent legal requirement. But consider this: Would a translated version of your online materials help LEP constituents obtain the same level of access to information as your English speaking constituents? If the answer is yes, then the materials should be translated.

ASK AN EXPERT: Where do you see the language services industry in 5 years?

Dr. Nitish Singh (Ph.D. MBA, MA), Brand2Global Program Leader (Global Digital Marketing & Localization Certification)

I see 2 groups of localization companies emerge: one group following the old ways of competing based on translation, and the other group competing based on rare and inimitable capabilities I mentioned in the previous answer. The future of most industries, including language services, will be disrupted or challenged by Artificial Intelligence, Ubiquitous Computing, Crowd-sourcing, Cloud computing, and emergence of new service models. Most importantly the language industry will be impacted by the dual trend toward acceleration in globalization and the reechoing of creolization, as a reactionary force against the pressures of globalization, so as to reassert national identity.

A couple of quick tips:

Providing your vendor with editable source documents will save time and money. You might think you are doing your vendor a favor by converting large files to PDFs, but it actually makes your project more difficult and may cost you more. Instead, always be sure to send the original source files from whatever application your document was created in. This could be Word, InDesign, Adobe Illustrator, Quark, Publisher, Articulate, PageMaker, FrameMaker, Excel, or any of a hundred others. A skilled vendor can easily work with all of them.

Talk to your project manager and account manager. If you have ideas or questions, make sure to tell the team you hired. Ideally, your LSP will use that feedback to create solutions and customized workflows.

Don't stress about criticism during the review process. Translation projects are naturally collaborative. A good vendor will listen to your feedback and may offer a critique as well. Remember that a better vendor will have a team of highly qualified translators and other staff who carefully review translations prior to sending the finished product to you. When or if criticism arises, don't forget that the best vendors will have processes to review varying opinions, errors and preferences, and resolve them.

Know the demographics of your constituents. When it's time to translate into Chinese, for example, be aware that there are two primary character sets for writing Chinese. "Simplified" Chinese is primarily used by people from the People's Republic of China (i.e., "mainland" China) and Singapore, while Traditional Chinese is used by people from The Republic of China (Taiwan) and Hong Kong. But be advised that even a translation done by someone from Hong Kong may not be acceptable to someone from Taiwan as the styles can be very different.

English is just another language. Think about this. While the character sets from other languages might seem strange or pretty or just plain confusing to an English speaker, immigrants may feel the same way about English! Keep this in mind when working on projects aimed at non-English speaking populations.

Use plain English whenever possible. Vague and opaque English will be equally confusing in other languages. Because of this, shorter, simpler English or "plain English" becomes even more important when translating your content into other languages. Remember, using "plain English" will save you money, shorten timelines, and make your message clearer.

Language access can begin with you. If your agency has never engaged a translation vendor or you see gaps in your current outreach programs, it's never too late to get involved. Ask your supervisor if you have a translation vendor and, if you don't, ask what is required to hire one.

Avoid the "Blame Game." Many of the LEP people your agency supports are striving to learn English—studying ESL books at home at night, or during work breaks. Until their language proficiency improves, translations bridge the gap. Remember, it's not their fault they don't speak English fluently, just like it's not your fault if you don't speak Portuguese!

CHAPTER 12

Take It to the Bank, Banco or 银行: Translation for Financial Institutions

As every banker knows, retail banking has become an extremely competitive business. Not only does it seem like are there bank branches on every corner, nowadays we also see ATMs in every mall and gas station, micro branches in most supermarkets, and there are many new online and mobile options. In fact, soldiers who are deployed in combat zones are even able to use their smartphones to deposit checks back home. There are also prepaid cards for those who resist traditional banking and, for elite consumers with bank accounts across the globe, private banking and luxury financial advisory start-ups to cater to them.

So ... how do financial institutions get ahead of the pack and stay there in such a competitive environment? One of the best ways commercial banks, credit unions, and other businesses that offer financial services can grow their customer base is to cater to non-English speakers. Because of shifting demographics, in many neighborhoods limited English proficient (LEP) speakers comprise a significant portion of the residents. In some areas, they are also more affluent than their English-speaking neighbors.

Multilingual Marketing for 'Unbanked' and High Net Worth Consumers

In the United States, immigrants are arriving from all parts of the world. In 2015, according to Nielsen Research, the fastest growing segment in the United States was from Asia, but Latinos from South and Central America, Africans, and most recently refugees from the Middle East are arriving every day too. It is easy to see how important these new populations can be to a financial institution's success. For example, nearly 79 percent of Asian Americans in the United States are foreign born and their buying power is expected to reach $1 trillion by 2018. As Chinese, Filipino, Indian, Korean and Japanese immigrants start new lives in the US, they will establish relationships with financial institutions. But which bank will they choose?

We believe these new Americans will choose the bank that is most effective at communicating their value proposition to them. Studies show that a full 50 percent of the non-native English speakers watching English language TV would prefer to do so in their native language.[1] This demonstrates that while these new immigrants may outwardly appear to be fully assimilated, many feel more comfortable absorbing messaging in their native language and, in fact, prefer it. If your organization isn't translating its messaging into Spanish, Chinese, and other languages, you are likely missing out on a lucrative new market.

Many financial institutions see LSPs as a vital partner for courting this attractive segment of the population. A high net worth customer may generate $200,000 or more in annual fees for a bank, so the motivation for wooing these elite customers, whether or not they speak English fluently, is substantial. On the flip side, LSPs can also help financial services organizations connect with the millions of ethnic or multicultural consumers who do not have a bank account. FDIC estimates that 9.6 million households in the United States are "unbanked." While financial services are commonly accessed by many within the LEP community, there are millions who remain "unbanked," living in a cash economy.

A number of cultural and sociopolitical factors deter multicultural consumers from depositing money into banks. Time and again, we see that directing "unbanked" consumers to regular financial institutions benefits these consumers in the long run, giving them a place to save money responsibly and avoid the fees that check cashing operations charge for services. In-language marketing to "unbanked" LEP Americans can drive new relationships.

---

1   Lo, Betty and Rosenberg, Seth, "Asian Americans: Culturally Connected and Forging the Future," The Asian-American Consumer 2015 Report, Nielsen Diverse Intelligence Series.

Dan Johnson

Communication is fundamental, and perhaps the most powerful tool we bipeds have at our disposal. Channels and media for communication have increased exponentially since the late 1990's when I began working in the industry. While language and languages continue to slowly evolve, the volume of communication and how we do so has exploded. Today, virtually anyone, anywhere can communicate globally using commonly available technology. No matter what language, what media, or what time of day, we can help solve the language piece of the communication puzzle. And that's pretty cool.

Is Translation Necessary?

Let's answer this question quickly: Yes! Financial institutions always need to understand a customer's financial standing and qualifications, and oftentimes translations are essential to get this key information. For example, if a borrower has brokerage statements from an investment advisor in Beijing, the US-based lender may have to translate these documents to determine whether the applicant qualifies for the loan he or she wants. Or if an individual wants to open a bank account in the United States but only has a French driver's license for identification, it too will need to be translated.

There are legal reasons that drive translations as well. Whether an LEP is shopping for credit or simply opening a retail bank account, there are countless policies, laws and regulatory guidelines that regulate the discussions conducted by licensed financial services providers and ultimately shape linguistic behavior.

Some of the main questions financial service providers who engage with LEPs need to ask:

- Does the LEP consumer understand what he/she is buying?
- Does the LEP consumer understand what he/she is investing in or the terms of the loan?
- Does the LEP consumer understand all the conditions and commitments associated with the financial product or service?

In the United States, it is always a good idea to provide verbal language support and documentation in the consumer's native language. Laws vary state by state, but delivering in-language documentation can protect a financial institution from possible fines and penalties from regulators. Each bank's legal staff is the best source for understanding the regulations related to translation.

Finally, some banks want to know if providing "high quality" translations is essential. Once again, this is a question for your internal legal and compliance team, but we believe the answer is that they are absolutely essential. Logically, if you forgo using high quality "native level" translators, your loan committee could potentially make a bad credit decision and issue a large loan to an unqualified borrower. Similarly, if your multicultural marketing brochures contain errors or are poorly translated, it could cause misunderstandings or damage the reputation of your organization within the LEP community. These scenarios are unappealing to say the least, and, luckily, preventable if you choose a reliable translation and localization partner.

Typical Stakeholders for Translation and Retail Banking

Inside a retail bank, when team members require translation support for print or digital use, it is essential to choose a trusted, reliable language service vendor who can deliver high quality translations, on time, every time. More importantly, using a professional translation company can increase compliance levels if the vendor offers secure, encrypted protocols for transferring files and documents.

The bank employees who most frequently require written translation support are:

- mortgage bankers
- mortgage underwriters
- retail bankers
- investment advisors
- loan processors

This list, while not comprehensive, offers a snapshot of the personnel who often interact with LEP or multicultural consumers. Just like native English speakers, LEP consumers turn to banks for buying a home, refinancing a mortgage, establishing a bank account, or getting a credit card.

Localizing Hotlines, Websites and Mobile Applications

All the largest banks in the US are competing for relationships with multicultural consumers. Along with visiting retail banks and ATM machines, these consumers interact with financial institutions through many pathways, including:

- customer service hotlines
- bank websites
- mobile applications
- online chat

At each of these touch points, the consumer experience should be uncomplicated and sensible to increase the likelihood of building a new relationship, or maintaining an existing one. One of the ways banks do this is by communicating in their clients' preferred language.

Increasingly, banks are investing in translation for websites and mobile applications, too. This trend shows no sign of stopping. Typically, these mobile applications and other digital assets are created by third party financial developers who manage the creation and updates of digital assets, collaborate with stakeholders in the bank and oftentimes, language service providers as well, throughout the development lifecycle. Overseas, the market for localization of mobile financial applications will increase exponentially over the next decade. In 2014, McKinsey reported there are 670 million digital banking consumers in Asia, and this number may grow to as many as 1.7 billion by 2020.[2]

Also, now that "chat" or "online advisors" are commonplace on consumer banking websites, it is likely that demand for real-time translation of these interactions will increase too. Some LSPs are experimenting with machine translation to support chat, but the quality of the output is generally inadequate. Much better quality will be achieved by using humans to support these sessions, but to be viable the translators must be online and available when needed. At LanguageLine, we believe that companies who employ thousands of professional linguists (like us) are the only ones who will be able to effectively meet this challenge.

---

[2] McKinsey and Company, "Digital Banking in Asia: Winning approaches in a new generation of financial services," 2014 report.

ASK AN EXPERT:

What does quality mean?

Dr. Nitish Singh (Ph.D. MBA, MA), Brand2Global Program Leader (Global Digital Marketing & Localization Certification)

Quality from the translation perspective is about conveying identical meaning or equivalency in meaning. Thus, translation quality is about vocabulary, conceptual, idiomatic equivalence. Quality from a broader context of Digital Localization is about creating communications and interfaces that really resonate with consumer's values and beliefs and meet their locale-specific aesthetic and functional requirements.

Rachael Cazden

I believe that now, today, in this modern era, more than ever, we need to try and communicate with each other so we may understand one another. We are not different races. We are one race, the human race. It doesn't matter where you were born, since, for the most part, we all want the same thing: peace, happiness, and prosperity. By communicating with each other, and finding common ground, we can honestly make the world a better place for the whole human race. So, let's chat.

Security: A Critical Component of Vendor Selection

One of the most essential priorities for any financial services organization is keeping customer data safe. If you work for a financial services business and have ever had to engage translation vendors, it is likely that you already know security levels at LSPs vary significantly. Security includes not only physical security over access to offices, server equipment, back-up media, and the like, but also how the LSPs handle data and digital records as well.

When evaluating the latter, most banking institutions focus on how projects are dispatched to their translation vendor and subsequently returned. As such, the typical questions they ask include: Are file transfers secure? Is the data encrypted? Do you offer a secure web portal or TMS (see Chapter 16)?

But this line of inquiry misses half the story. What most vendors don't discuss, and most clients don't know to question is: What happens after the LSP has received your project? It is very common for translators, formatters, and engineers to be located in different locations from the project manager, so be sure to ask tough questions about how your vendor handles "internal" transfers between all of the various parties that might work on your project.

One final thought. It's important to understand that the vast majority of LSPs have less than 20 employees, and more commonly, less than 10 employees. Given this, it is highly likely that they do not have the IT resources, and therefore the procedures and controls, to pass a comprehensive IT audit. Data security and protecting Personally Identifiable Information (PII) is critical. The only way to be certain that your customers' vital information is secure is to partner with a vendor who offers intensive security, expert employees, and a long track record of supporting financial institutions.

Don't Be Left Behind

As financial institutions compete for multicultural and limited English speaking customers, we are increasingly seeing forms and large signs inside banks in Spanish, Chinese, Arabic and many other languages. Across the world, ATM machines now offer menus in two or more languages, as do mobile applications.

At LanguageLine, we are also seeing growing demand for all modalities of language services, including translation, localization, over the phone interpretation, video remote interpretation, and face-to-face interpretation. The cost of using a video remote interpreter to facilitate a conversation, for example, is negligible compared to the profits gained from keeping a wealthy client. Video remote interpretation is not just useful—it's an opportunity to impress your customers with cutting edge technology, giving the presentation a "wow factor" that dazzles clients. Similarly, although less fun but still essential, providing certified translations for an elite client is a small cost to pay if it helps win a lucrative new account. Welcoming customers from many countries is good for financial enterprises.

Chapter 13

Side Effects May Include Higher Patient Satisfaction, Reduced Costs, and Better Health Outcomes - Language Access for Health Care Organizations

Overview/Introduction

As the United States becomes increasingly diverse, ensuring effective communication for the nation's growing limited English proficient (LEP) population is no longer an option—it's a necessity. For health care organizations, the surge in the newly insured LEP population coupled with the Affordable Care Act's emphasis on patient satisfaction and quality care makes the need all the more urgent. Translation is a vital, but often overlooked, component of effective language access plans.

The Affordable Care Act – Impact on Health Care Providers

At the heart of the Affordable Care Act (ACA) is the desire to reduce costs by shifting the emphasis away from the amount of care provided and towards the quality of the care provided. A number of financial incentives were put in place to align the behaviors of health care providers with this goal. Two of these mechanisms include tying Medicare reimbursements to readmission rates and issuing bonuses or penalties to providers based on patient satisfaction levels. Both are directly impacted by the translation of health care documentation.

Patient Education Materials and Readmission Rates

Starting in 2013, the Centers for Medicare and Medicaid Services (CMS) began phasing in penalties for providers with high 30-day readmission rates. In addition to assessing penalties, the cost of caring for the patient during the readmission is not reimbursable.

Two of the most common reasons cited for avoidable readmissions are language barriers and health literacy challenges. To reduce readmission rates and improve health outcomes, LEP patients should be provided with proper translation of important educational materials at an appropriate health literacy level. At a minimum, health care providers need to make certain that all of their patients, including LEPs, understand:

- Their illness,
- Procedures they are undergoing,
- Their specific disease(s) and medical condition(s),
- Treatment and follow-up care, and
- How to maintain health and wellness.

The Guide to Translation and Localization

Improving Patient Satisfaction Levels

Another mechanism put into place under the ACA is an emphasis on patient satisfaction. Nearly $1 billion in annual payments are now tied to patient satisfaction levels. The top performing health care providers are rewarded with bonuses and the lower performers are assessed penalties.

To gauge patient satisfaction, a survey called the HCAHPS (Hospital Consumer Assessment of Healthcare Providers and Systems) is administered to patients, who are asked a series of questions regarding the quality of the care they received. A significant number (41%) of the questions specifically ask about communication between the patient and the provider. Predictably, LEP patients report much lower satisfaction rates (36% lower) compared to English speaking patients and are 47% more likely not to return for future care.

Consistently communicating with an LEP patient in their native language is crucial to improving HCAHPS scores and patient satisfaction levels. While most health care organizations provide interpreters for their LEP patients, written documentation is usually offered only in English. Throughout a typical patient experience, there are multiple touchpoints where communication occurs in written format (See Figure 1). If these materials are not translated, communication with the LEP patient suffers ... as do HCAHPS scores and patient satisfaction levels.

Triage

- Permission to Treat
- Insurance

Admitting

- Notice of Patient Rights
- HIPAA Notification
- Financial Documents
- Informational Brochures
- Insurance

MD

- Informed Consent
- Referrals to Aftercare
- Treatment
- Medication Education

Testing

- Specific Consents
- Informed Consent

Pharmacy

- Medication Information
- Insurance

Discharge

- Discharge Instructions
- Information for Transfer
- Medication Education
- Patient Education

Figure 1: Documents at Point of Contact

Translation of Vital Documents – It's the Law

In addition to the changes implemented under the ACA, health care providers are required to translate documents deemed "vital" to a patient's care. To determine whether a document is considered a vital document, organizations apply a four factor test:

- Number or percentage of LEP patients in the patient population,
- Frequency of contact with the LEP patient,
- Importance of the service(s) being provided, and
- Resources available and cost to the provider.

Health care providers should have a process in place to identify all of the vital documents that need to be translated. These typically include:

- Patient forms,
- Discharge instructions,
- Information about language assistance,
- Complaint forms,
- Notices of eligibility criteria for, rights in, denial or loss of, or decreases in, benefits or services, and
- Intake forms that may have clinical consequences.

Best Practices for Health Care Translations

The importance of providing translated materials to LEP patients cannot be overemphasized. Nevertheless, many health care organizations are left wondering how to expand their language access programs to include translation. When implementing translation services, there are several best practices that should be considered.

Centralization

The most effective translation programs start with a centralized process. Translation requests should be channeled through a specific department (such as Interpretation Services) or specific individuals at the department level. It is a good idea to centralize requests in order to validate the need,

Cory Markert

Traveling around the country to support our health care clients has allowed me to see firsthand the direct impact our services have on patients. Whether we are translating educational materials for patients with chronic conditions, a website to make information available in-language or discharge instructions for patients being released from the hospital, we truly do improve the lives of patients every day!

reduce duplicate requests and manage translation budgets. For vital documents, most health care providers set up a formal committee that meets on a regular basis to identify documents that match the vital documents criteria and therefore should be translated into the threshold languages.

Internal Resources

External translation agencies usually handle the bulk of the translation work but internal resources (bilingual staff, translators, interpreters, etc.) also play a vital role in the process. Internal staff is most often utilized to translate very small or urgent requests such as discharge instructions and to provide feedback regarding terminology and style preferences. Most importantly, internal staff often perform a final verification of translations produced by outside translation agencies. Before calling upon internal resources, it is important to test and verify the bilingual competency and subject matter expertise of staff members.

External Resources

Health care providers understand there are many benefits to relying on outside translation agencies. Outside agencies will have expertise that is not available to most health care organizations, including linguists for hundreds of languages and linguists with specialized subject matter expertise like cardiology or pediatrics. Also, even though outside agencies only ever use professional translators, the best language service vendors will use multiple linguists on every project to check each other's work.

In comparison, health care providers that rely on internal resources rarely use a second translator to check the work of the first. External vendors will also perform other quality assurance procedures to check formatting, confirm that all text was translated and, if there is ever any doubt, review by a third linguist to ensure a high quality deliverable. Due to the comprehensive translation process used by most agencies, certified translations that shifts the liability to the external agency should a problem arise with a translated document are also available. Lastly, turnaround times are almost always faster and more reliable when using an external language service provider, particularly for larger and more complex documents.

Health Literacy

Health literacy refers to a patient's ability to obtain, read and understand health care information. When translating content in the health care industry, health literacy needs to be taken into consideration. Simply providing a translated version of a document does not ensure a patient will comprehend the material. Health literacy levels may fluctuate depending upon the demographics of the patient population, but as a general rule, a 4th to 6th grade reading level should be used to ensure patients can understand the information. For best results, we recommend creating the English source materials using the same reading level that you require for the translated documents.

Conclusion

Health care providers are seeing increasingly diverse patient populations, and effective communication is of paramount importance to the quality of care they receive. Recent regulations have both directly and indirectly affected the need to provide translated documentation to patients. By utilizing the best practices detailed above, health care organizations can consistently provide high quality translations that will be understood by their LEP patients and will address deficiencies with patient education while increasing patient satisfaction levels.

Chapter 14

Localization Engineering

Engineering

The processing power of computers has doubled every two years for nearly five decades. This observation, generally referred to as Moore's Law, confirms just how fast modern technology advances and is indicative of the growing influence that technology has in most aspects of life, likely including the way you do business. In turn, rapid technological growth presents language service providers with two distinct challenges. First, it means LSPs must keep pace with an increasingly sophisticated and powerful array of translation-related computing tools. Second, it means that localization buyers are constantly employing new development platforms, new file formats, and other emerging technologies that their localization workflows will need to accommodate. These realities make localization engineering one of the most important components of the localization process. After all, it is a localization engineer who has the expertise and technological savvy to break these complex projects down into manageable pieces and then put them back together like nothing happened. Except now your application, your website, and your interactive eLearning content work flawlessly in multiple languages!

Perhaps right now you are thinking, "Oh boy, I'm no engineer and it sounds like this chapter is going to be chock full of technical details! Do I really need to understand this all myself?" The short answer is no. The most important thing to take away from this chapter can be summarized by the following sentence:

It is essential to the long-term value of your localization investment that your vendor has the knowledge, expertise, and resources to meet your future needs and keep up with the latest technology and specialized tools.

As straightforward as this may sound, fewer and fewer LSPs these days actually employ localization engineers. Instead, they outsource this important function or try to rely exclusively on tools to do the tasks that engineers have historically performed. The next chapter will discuss the new tools that are available to LSPs and how they can indeed make light work of many complicated tasks. But in the end, there's simply no substitute for the added value that a strong engineering team can provide.

If you care to know more about the details of localization engineering and the types of projects where experienced engineers are important, then keep reading! Otherwise, you've already learned just about everything you need to know, and you can leave the nuts and bolts of this chapter for those in your staff who actually manage and maintain the technology behind your products and services. Just make sure that someone is ready to ask potential vendors the tough questions needed to ensure that your project is a success.

From Day One – Get Set Before You Typeset

When companies develop products with only one language in mind (usually English), the process of localization often reveals a lot of unexpected hurdles. For example, if you set character limits for certain UI elements, such as a clickable button, based solely on the length of your English strings, what happens when the equivalent Russian or Spanish text expands by 20%? Or let's say you choose a character encoding for your program that works just fine for English, but isn't able to display the accented letters of Turkish or the characters of Thai. If you're making assumptions that all languages behave the same way as you develop your product, you can easily and unwittingly make functional elements of your product dependent on the structure and behavior of one particular language, which can lead to major problems down the road.

Some examples of common development practices that are problematic for localization include ***string concatenation*** (recombining individual words or phrases to create larger strings), ***string re-use*** (using the same instance of a single string in multiple places), and the use of ***placeholder variables*** to create

The Guide to Translation and Localization

Viktoriya Voznyuk

My country of origin is Ukraine. I speak three languages and have spent some time in seven countries. If you asked me how many languages from how many countries I have worked with since joining LLTS in 2011—it's more than I thought was possible. And growing.

multiple versions of a sentence from a common "stem." During development, these practices may seem like clever efficiencies. Why create additional, unique resources when you just need a string that's already used elsewhere repeatedly? Why write multiple versions of what is essentially the same sentence save for one word? Why write a new string to be localized when you already have the translations for each word in that sentence? In all these scenarios, however, you're making the grave mistake of assuming that what works for one language will work for all others.

For example in English, the word "complete" can be used as an adjective or a verb, and the same instance of this string could be used in both contexts in your application without consequence. As a result, you might be tempted to translate just one instance of the word "complete" and try to use that translation in all the different contexts where the English word is found (such as in a button prompting a user to "complete" an action and as a status indicating that some other action is "complete"). In Spanish, however, not only are the verb-form and adjective-form of this word different, but the adjective could be written four different ways depending on what word modifies (taking into account gender, and number). Suddenly, what worked reliably in English becomes a game of chance in Spanish and you're likely to be left with a translation that is only correct in certain situations. In reality you should create and localize a separate instance of each repeated word so that linguists can adjust each translation for a particular context.

For reasons like these, localization engineers are often brought in well before there's anything ready to translate to develop the product in such a way that it can be easily adapted for export to any country or locale. Addressing the linguistic limitations of your design after localization begins, or worse, after the original product is supposed to be final, can be expensive and time consuming. In many cases, an early meeting with a qualified localization engineer can save time and reduce localization costs in the future.

In addition to providing guidance on encoding, string management, and overall design and layout, localization engineers can help with several other important issues:

- Does the design account for cultural differences in various metrics such as currency, units of measure, date format, phone numbers, and addresses?
- Is all the text you want translated accessible (externalized) and/or isolated from other code for easy extraction?
- Do automatically sorted lists take into account differences in the target locale? For example, if the original list is sorted alphabetically in English, these items are likely to appear "out of order" after translation.

A consultation with an experienced engineer is a very cost-effective way to ensure that your product is ready for localization—especially when measured against the delays and costs associated with trying to resolve these issues during the localization process. While a thorough internationalization review will not necessarily rid your files of all potential localization headaches, it will reduce them to a manageable level and prevent the introduction of additional defects during the localization process. In general, the more interaction between your engineering department and your translation vendor's engineering team in the early stages of the project, the fewer issues there will be to fix later on.

On Our Way: Localization Begins

Once all preliminary localization issues have been addressed, the localization process can begin on a good foundation. And how does a localization engineer contribute once translation is ready to begin? Most projects start with the engineer isolating and extracting translatable text strings (commonly referred to as assets or resources) from the source content, and preparing specialized files that facilitate translation without disturbing the integrity of the source files. From there, the next step is to analyze that text using Computer Aided Translation (CAT) tools and a Translation Memory (TM), which are discussed in detail in the next chapter, to determine how much leveraging is available so that a budget and timeline can be prepared.

For basic project types this process can mostly be automated, and some LSPs have even built this functionality into their Translation Management Systems. For more complex projects however, maximizing the leveraging from TM tools requires the expert attention and manual effort of a localization engineer. The engineer's approach will vary depending on file types and the nature of the project. Here are some common project types and a description of the efforts involved for each.

Zoe Nyman

I'm known as the "runner" in the Portland office, even in high heels. Outside of work, I do my running near where I live, averaging 16-18 miles a week these days. A firm believer in an active lifestyle, I try my best to exercise and eat right. My goal is to keep active and be able to hike well into my 70's or 80's.

Page by Page: Documentation

Localizing basic documentation is the least complicated process for an engineer. In fact, for some of the new TM applications on the market, it is just a matter of importing and exporting text to and from files created via a desktop publishing application or content management system (CMS). As a result of the functionality these tools offer, many vendors no longer employ engineers and, instead, rely on project managers to prep files. This is not without ramifications. Project managers seldom have the skills and expertise to troubleshoot and work around problems when things don't go exactly as planned, which, like anything in life, is often. An engineer can not only resolve issues on the fly, but also recognizes in advance other potential stumbling blocks that other contributors may face downstream.

Stop the Presses: Help File Localization

Print documentation is quickly losing ground to interactive help systems. Well-structured online help provides users with incredible search capability, allowing them to find more information in less time than with conventional print documentation. Many help users say this leads to a richer experience.

Single source publishing tools such as Author-it, Flare, Arbortext, WebWorks ePublisher, or RoboHelp now allow you to create these interactive help systems quickly, easily, and inexpensively. But with each of these systems comes a wide variety of complicated file sets to be localized. The main help formats being used are WinHelp, HTML Help, WebHelp, JavaHelp, Oracle Help, and FlashHelp. Each of these formats has its own specific uses and characteristics, but the process to localize any of them starts with extracting translatable text. The appropriate method for doing so depends on the particular application used to author the help content, and generally requires the expertise of a Localization Engineer.

ASK AN EXPERT:

How will new technologies reshape the role of human translators?

Laura Brandon, GALA Executive Director

Translators will continue to be vital to our industry's progress, even as new technologies emerge. Increased automation diminishes the need for skills like plain text translating and manual handling of files. But machines can't yet replace human intuition and judgment, making it likely that translators will be relied upon for sector and cultural matters, contextualization of content, and quality evaluation. Furthermore, as newer technologies facilitate direct collaboration between the linguist and client, we may see more organizations work directly with translators rather than relying on language service providers for project management services.

Interface This: Software Localization

Not surprisingly, the wide variety of programming languages and platform combinations used in software development today can make for a very complicated localization project. For vendors with limited technical expertise, the jargon and terminology alone can seem overwhelming: Is it a Windows-based application? OS X? UNIX? Linux? iOS? Android? Symbian? Mainframe? Java? Is it web-based? Server-based? Client-based? Cloud-based?

These questions underscore yet again the importance of choosing a vendor with the engineering expertise to take on your software localization project.

The above notwithstanding, software localization projects still begin with the most basic of engineering tasks. You guessed it: isolating the text from the application for translation. Most translators wouldn't know where to begin with a software project and the unusual file types that come with it, so they rely on an engineer to make their work more manageable. In some cases, that means isolating the text from the underlying code, creating a special file for the translator, and then putting it all back together unharmed when the translation is done. In other cases, the localization engineer will set the project up with a proprietary tool or an off-the-shelf application like Catalyst, Passolo, or Multilizer that allows the translator to work directly on compiled files and executables. All things being equal, however, the former approach is more common and minimizes the amount of preparation needed, reducing the potential for defects being introduced during the localization process.

Going World Wide: Web Localization

Web-based user interfaces are increasingly popular because they are easier to maintain and offer more support than client-based applications. In most cases, both web-based applications and commercial websites have a database such as Oracle, SQL Server, MySQL or, in rare cases, Access, as the back end. One of the most compelling advantages of a database-backed website is the downstream benefit. Updates, including localization maintenance, become very easy and very cheap since accessing and replacing the content is simple. With client-based applications, on the other hand, end users must replace the outdated version of their software with an updated copy for the changes to appear.

In general, websites built with dynamic content are usually very localization-friendly from an engineering perspective. No matter the type of database supporting a website or web-based application, the primary objective for the engineer is still to sort out what needs to be translated and what does not. If the database is well organized, it is relatively easy to extract the text strings using a well-defined spec sheet that lists the localizable resources. It is worth noting, though, that some programming languages, or a combination of programming languages, can make it a little more difficult to extract localizable resources when generating files for the linguists. An experienced engineer, familiar with the most common languages used in web development, will need to navigate any technical issues and ensure the job is done right.

More recently, a number of "proxy" solutions have emerged, which eliminate the need to deal with source files and allow translators to work directly "within" a copy of your website. With traditional web localization, the translated versions of your site reside on your servers and any changes need to be identified and tracked by you; with proxy solutions the translated versions of your website reside in the cloud. See Chapter 17 for more information about one such product.

Multimedia Localization

Finally, another project type with many "moving parts" that usually requires the additional expertise of a localization engineer is multimedia localization. Multimedia materials can contain video, audio, text, still images, and/or complex graphics. Incidentally, the word "multimedia" itself is a reflection of what localization engineering really is: a little bit of everything.

Examples of this type of project include eLearning, video games, interactive software, web applications, DVDs, and kiosks. They can be used for virtually any purpose, such as entertainment, sales and marketing, training, or education, and they can be produced in a wide variety of applications that use many different formats:

- Adobe Premiere
- Adobe After Effects
- Articulate Storyline
- Articulate Studio
- Camtasia

With so many variable components and options available, the multimedia localization process calls for additional skill sets to handle audio or video text adaptation, voiceover recording, and even software engineering.

As expected, the project starts with an engineer extracting the necessary text for translation, but once that's done there may be additional steps unique to multimedia projects. If your material has voiceover audio, the translated script must be recorded and the audio engineered to the right specs. That audio then has to be synced with some video footage or animation, often with the help of a linguist. Even if you're just doing subtitles, at a minimum, the reassembly involves placing any on-screen text into position in the localized files while paying special attention not to alter any color specifications, system fonts, text attributes, code, scripting, navigation features or interactive text.

A sign in a Japanese airport

Conclusion

The latest generation of translation memory tools has essentially automated the process for extracting text from source files and then calculating leveraging. The direct result is that fewer and fewer LSPs employ their own engineers. While it's true that the primary objective for an engineer is to safely extract the text from your files for translation, there are many variables that can make this task harder than it sounds. So although automation may work for simple files, it often doesn't work—or doesn't work well—with complex files.

It is also important to understand that not all leveraging calculations are equal. At LanguageLine, we believe that by customizing the file prep process according to the specifications and characteristics of each project, highly skilled localization engineers are able to achieve higher leveraging than what the tools can achieve on their own.

Hopefully this chapter has illustrated why it is still essential that your vendor has the appropriate in-house engineering resources to execute any type of project you might have. In the next chapter we will discuss some of the tools that engineers use.

A sign in Israel

Chapter 15

Translation Memory and Terminology Management

"Tools of the trade"

Chapter 14 highlighted the importance of choosing a vendor with an experienced in-house engineering team. In this chapter, we will explore the tools that localization engineers use when working on your projects, the advantages they provide, and what their limitations are.

Translation Memories

Translation Memory (TM) technology has only been commercially available since the mid-1990s. Today, however, this technology is used by almost every translation vendor and is as important to how translators carry out their jobs as email is to office workers.

Conceptually, it's easiest to think of a Translation Memory as a database in which some source text (English, usually) is stored side by side with its equivalent in a different language. The bilingual data is maintained in discrete chunks called Translation Units (TUs) and organized in such a way that you can compare new content with what's already been translated, and identify matches. It is also possible to attach metadata to each TU, such as the originating project name and number, or any other type of information that can further refine your translations and improve leveraging; but this will likely require selecting a vendor with localization engineering capabilities rather than one who relies on their PMs to manage TMs.

Over time, every new translation project will add to the future value of your TM because, as your TM grows in size, you are more likely to find matches with existing TUs. And in the end, nearly all vendors will allow you to pay less to translate content that is matched in your TM. Even if you're starting with a blank TM and paying the full per-word price at first, you will begin to see cost savings after just one project when working with a professional language service company.

CAT Tools

Since a Translation Memory is essentially just a storage container, it's not much use without additional tools to take advantage of what's in there. Computer Aided Translation (CAT) Tools are software programs that work in conjunction with Translation Memories and provide a streamlined working environment for translators. There are many tools available in the marketplace, each with its own features, but all serve the same primary purpose.

When new content is submitted for translation it is typically analyzed using a CAT Tool to determine both the total number of words that need to be translated and whether any of that text has been translated before. The degree to which new content matches the existing translations that are stored in the TM is called "Leveraging." CAT Tools generally classify the "matches" they find into three categories: 100% Matches, Fuzzy text, and New text. 100% matches are self-explanatory, but CAT Tools are also looking for "partial" matches, which are scored for similarity on a scale of 0-99%. The cutoffs for each category vary from vendor to vendor, but it's common to see matches of 85% and below counted as new text, and matches of 86-99% counted as fuzzy text. In some cases, it may even be possible to achieve better than a 100% match since CAT tools can also consider the strings that come before and after. If a matched string occurs between the same two strings that it did the first time it was processed, it's considered to be a context match, a.k.a. an ICE match or a 101% match.

While the leveraging analysis will be expressed as a word count, broken down by category with a certain number of words in each, it's important to understand that the tools are actually comparing "segments" rather than individual words. Segments can be thought of as a catchall term that could refer to a complete sentence, a phrase, or yes, even a single word. As new content is analyzed by the CAT tool, the text is "segmented" according to rules that are part of the software's code, and it's those segments that are compared to other, previously translated segments in the TM. Generally speaking, CAT Tools use both standard punctuation (like periods) and other formatting information (like line breaks) to decide when a segment begins and ends. Once your content has been separated into segments, it can be compared to the TM.

It should be noted that when content is analyzed for similarity to what's been translated before, meaning is not taken into account at all. The tools are simply comparing sequences of characters to identify potential matches. Consider the information in the table below:

Original Segment	New Segment	Match Percentage
The conference room will not be available for the rest of the week.	The conference room will be available for the rest of the week.	~99%, but opposite in meaning
John is heavier than Mary.	Mary weighs less than John.	<10%, but nearly identical in meaning
James and his brother walk their dogs in the park often.	James and his brother walk their dogs in the park frequently.	~99%, and nearly identical in meaning

To a CAT Tool, the segments in the first row are far more similar than the sentences in the second row, even though in the first row, the meaning of the two is opposite while the two in the second row are essentially paraphrases of each other. Contrast these with the sentences in the third row where neither the form nor the meaning changes very much from version A to version B. These subtleties are important because as a translator works through the content, the CAT Tool presents the translation associated with each match as a suggested starting point for translating the new segment. For the "dogs in the park" example, the translator could potentially accept the partial match without any modification and use the same translation for both versions of the sentence. In the first case, however, the matched translation will be completely wrong without a minor, but critical, change from the translator.

Even when a 100% match is found in the TM, additional editing by the translator may be warranted due to contextual differences that change its meaning and cause the previous translation to be inappropriate. This is an important point to understand because some translation vendors don't review matches and it could be a reason that quotes can vary from one vendor to another. Nevertheless, it's fairly obvious how this matching system can save a translator time, especially if similar or identical strings are used frequently in your content. Moreover, since you're paying less per word for matched content, there are significant savings as well.

The preceding paragraphs laid out the benefits of building a robust TM. As is often the case, however, many buyers may already have thousands of words' worth of previously translated content, but no TM ... especially if their previous vendor did not maintain a TM or make it available to them. But fear not! By using any number of alignment tools, a localization engineer can create a TM for you if you have matching source and target versions of a file. These tools will independently segment the source and target files you have available, and then align corresponding segments to create new TUs. Beware, however, that this can be more complicated than it seems. Translations don't always keep a 1-to-1, string for string ratio with the source, so your best bet is to find a vendor with the engineering and linguistic resources to take on this task. Otherwise you can end up with falsely equivalent TUs which compromise the utility of the TM.

Translation Memory and Terminology Management

The other invaluable function that CAT Tools provide is to extract source text from its original file type or format and convert it into an XML-based file format that is universally compatible with the plethora of programs that are used by professional translators. This eliminates the need for linguists to master a multitude of applications or purchase a large library of expensive licenses in order to work on all of the different types of content they might receive. Instead, the CAT tool itself functions as a word processor of sorts that not only supports just about every conceivable type of file, but allows the translator to leverage the Translation Memory wherever possible. Rather than overwriting the original source text as each translation is completed, however, CAT Tools store both the source segment and the translated equivalent side by side, which is why these files are referred to as "bilingual." The content of the completed bilingual files can be saved into the TM to create new TUs for future matching.

A markup language such as XML (Extensible Markup Language) is a powerful system for annotating, organizing, and storing information (particularly text) in a format that is both machine- and user-friendly. This is especially important when it comes to localization because CAT Tools encode a great deal of information beyond the plain text that needs to be translated. For example, as the tools separate text from its original format, they essentially "remember" where each source string comes from in the original file and store this information in the file that is sent to the translator. Later, when the translation is completed, a localization engineer reconstructs the source file by using a CAT Tool to automatically swap out the original source string with its target equivalent from the bilingual file. This process is commonly known as "cleaning" a file. Once it's back in its original format, the "reconstructed" source file then goes on to subsequent stages of production, which vary depending on source file type and other project details.

Terminology Management

Aside from manipulating and organizing text strings and streamlining translation efforts, modern CAT Tools also help ensure that preferred terminology is used consistently in your translations through the use of glossaries and terminology lists. Typically, these lists, which can be monolingual or bilingual, contain all of the product-specific, company-specific, industry-specific, technical, or just plain difficult terms, along with their definitions, that translators need to know when translating. They may also include other important or frequently used terms too, including:

- selected operating environment terminology of major software developers (e.g., Microsoft),
- software and documentation that the client may have previously localized,
- other localized resource materials such as marketing collateral and product lists,
- company standards (such as part numbers, technical and product support information, warranties, license agreements, copyrights, references to other software programs, product names, brand names, and non-translated terms), and

ASK AN EXPERT:
How will new technologies reshape the role of human translators?

Dr. Nitish Singh (Ph.D. MBA, MA), Brand2Global Program Leader (Global Digital Marketing & Localization Certification)

The emergence of artificial intelligence and the developments in statistical and rule-based machine translation can transform the role of translators. I see translators taking up more of the role of being an editor and also a linguistic expert. Machines cannot yet decipher context specific or cultural nuances, and for that, we need human input.

ASK AN EXPERT:

What do you think will be the next largest area of growth in this industry?

Florian Faes, Slator Co-Founder

The next wave of growth in the language industry is likely to come from businesses who leverage the massive cloud-based resources in AI and machine learning and build solutions on top of it that solve real-life problems in the translation supply chain.

- country standards for expressing functional or cultural dictates such as publishing standards, sorting of lists, abbreviations, time, dates, holidays, currency, and measurements.

The chief purpose of the glossary is to guide the linguist in understanding the meaning and context for specialized terms so that they can, in turn, produce better translations. The terminology list, on the other hand, serves mainly to ensure consistency in the translation of all key terms, both within your content and with other, already translated content, by providing the linguist with the approved translation for each of the terms contained therein. This is helpful not only for obscure terms, but for common terms that might be translated multiple ways.

CAT Tools integrate these supplemental translation assets through terminology management modules that automatically flag any term that is located in the glossary. Not only do these modules ensure that the glossary is used whenever (and wherever) the key terms appear in the course of translation, they also minimize the time a linguist needs to go back and forth between reference materials and applications.

Glossary Development

If you have a lot of content to translate, and especially if you intend to establish a long term partnership with a vendor, developing a glossary early on is very important. There are several approaches you can employ. In some cases, you will know already which terms in your source content will need special consideration based on input from technical writers, software engineers, marketing departments, etc. Other times, what belongs on these lists is not so cut-and-dry, and developing them requires a little more effort. Using additional tools, localization engineers can analyze your content before translation begins and identify terminology candidates by considering factors including, but not limited to, the following:

- how frequently the term is repeated,
- how evenly the term is distributed throughout the content, and
- whether there is ambiguity about what the term means (it could be a common word that is appropriated for some other use, or means something else in a specific context).

After the list of key terms has been finalized, a team of translators with relevant expertise can begin researching the terms to come up with the best possible translations for your content. Ideally, the final, translated list is reviewed and approved by one of your in-country representatives before general translation begins. The use of an approved glossary and terminology list will ensure that your translations reflect your preferences and that your TM will be consistent and well organized from day one.

Translation Memory and Terminology Management

Conclusion

Effective utilization of modern CAT Tools is of paramount importance to a successful localization program. Not only will they improve translation quality by enhancing consistency both within and between documents, but reusing previously translated content will dramatically decrease localization costs by reducing the number of words that need to be translated in the first place.

It is also important to understand that the potential reduction in translation costs that can be realized from these tools far exceeds the penny or two per word you might save by shopping one vendor against another. Despite this, some localization firms assign the task of working with, managing, and maintaining TMs and glossaries to their project managers. While this might be appropriate on a small scale, the best vendors will use highly skilled localization engineers to ensure that their clients get maximum benefit from their translation assets. An inaccurate or corrupted TM (whether it is a linguistic corruption or an encoding corruption) can defeat the purpose of having one, adding to the cost of every project and ultimately hurting the quality of the translations.

Whether your company is in the Fortune 500 or a grassroots start-up, the quality and effectiveness of your TM and terminology assets will be best served by a localization partner who is continually integrating the latest tools and technology into the solutions they offer—and who also uses highly trained localization engineers to ensure that maximum benefit is achieved from them.

Oussama Abou-Jamous

I was fortunate I was born in one of the oldest cities in the world. Sidon (in South Lebanon) has been inhabited since sometime around 4000 B.C. by many different civilizations like the Assyrians, Babylonians, Egyptians, Persians, Greeks, Romans, Ottoman, Arabs. I guess this explains my interest in languages and meeting people from all over the world. I used to chase tourists visiting the city to practice my English which I thought was good until I moved to the US and landed in Houston. But the accent there was too hard for me to understand and I was told to move to the West Coast and that's how I landed in Portland and joined LanguageLine in 2006.

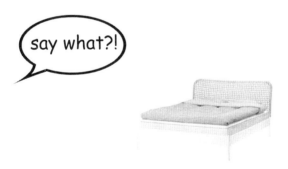

As the Wall Street Journal covered in 2012, Ikea has run into problems in the past with some of their product names taking on unintended meanings. The name 'Redalen' (one of their beds), for instance, also happens to be a town in Norway and vulgar slang term in Thailand. 'Jättebra', the name they gave a plant pot, will also raise a few Thai eyebrows.

CHAPTER 16

Translation Management Systems, Connectors, and Automation

Alphabet Soup – TMS, GMS, CMS

In today's business environment *automation* is the next frontier. Companies of every stripe are looking for ways to incorporate new technology into their workflows to increase productivity and reduce time to market. Although translation may jump out as an obvious candidate for automation, as you may recall from Chapter 3 of this book, Machine Translation tools have yet to realize their full commercial potential. As a result, many language service vendors have instead turned their attention to other aspects of production in their quest for increased automation.

Enter translation management systems (TMS), also known as globalization management systems (GMS). To some degree or another, all TMSs share these two objectives:

- reduce the time and cost associated with repetitive, nonessential tasks in the localization workflow, and
- filter out those tasks that require higher level analysis and creativity.

In other words, these applications often strive to automate all parts of a workflow except translation. Accordingly, a TMS might have features that facilitate file management, enable communication between stakeholders, convert text into a format that can be easily read by translation memory tools (aka "prepping files"), securely transfer files, improve translator efficiency, track financial information, streamline publishing, and can even host a vendor marketplace. They do so by connecting and integrating disparate technologies such as business systems, content management systems (CMS), computer aided translation (CAT) tools, and so forth. A robust translation management system keeps projects flowing by automatically linking all of the tasks and people involved in each step of a workflow.

Submit Locally; Manage Centrally

Not surprisingly, TMS tools come in all shapes and sizes. Some are sophisticated, stand-alone tools that are developed and licensed by technology vendors who specialize in this distinct market. Their applications offer lots of cool features and functionality, and will support the largest multinational organizations ... typically at a cost that will raise eyebrows. Others offer a narrower set of features and may complement another application such as a translation memory tool. Proprietary TMS systems also may be offered by larger LSPs for an additional fee or perhaps as a complimentary service in exchange for securing your translation business.

In our experience, smaller consumers of localization services are mostly interested in obtaining a good quality deliverable using an easy, straight forward workflow that allows them to exchange files via email or FTP. This simple approach is most appropriate for businesses that only need to translate content periodically. But depending on security requirements, how frequently you translate, the structure of your organization, and even your strategies for growth, a more sophisticated solution may be required. For example, as translation programs become larger and more complex, basic tasks such as identifying what content has changed and how much of that needs to be translated, locating the corresponding editable source files (so that you can provide them to your vendor), and transferring the files to and from your vendor can become time consuming and cumbersome. And at some point, without automation, these mundane tasks can quickly overwhelm your internal resources, who already have full time jobs doing other things.

The benefits of a robust Translation Management System become obvious if you consider how challenging it might be for a large multinational company to process all of their projects that could be submitted by thousands of potential requesters located throughout the world, and then monitor the status of each, wherever they originated, 24/7. The best TMSs are designed to do just that. In other words, they allow companies to manage all translation related activities with minimal administrative effort, usually through a centralized portal.

These portals, which are typically accessed via a web link, provide a secure, single point of entry into the translation workflow. This basic feature seems elementary, but when you have hundreds of users submitting projects from across the globe, it can eliminate a great deal of confusion over how and where to do it.

Furthermore, depending on how the drop site is configured, dispatching projects could be as simple as checking a few boxes and hitting send. In most cases, these systems will capture all the critical details, such as language and file type, and then immediately confirm that your files are queued up for translation. Compare the peace of mind this provides to a traditional email submission where you are left wondering if your project just ended up in someone's junk folder.

Uploading files to a secure, globally accessible portal offers numerous other advantages as well:

Sensitive messages and documents can't be inadvertently forwarded to the wrong email recipients;

Access to confidential data is only available to individuals who have been approved to see it;

Files remain available to everyone who needs them when they need them, so long as they have been granted access;

Version control is easier too as the TMS eliminates the need to constantly download and re-upload files with each handoff;

Files are maintained in a central, globally accessible location (which could be in the cloud on or a private server depending on the TMS), ensuring that files won't get trapped inside an email or on someone's local drive;

Comprehensive reporting of everything that has been submitted for translation is easily available, including project status, language, date submitted and date of completion.

ASK AN EXPERT:

What does language access mean now to your organization? In 5 years?

Winnie Heh, Career Advisor for Translation, Interpretation, and Localization Management at Middlebury Institute of International Studies at Monterey

As an educational institution, we closely monitor new talent needs in the language industry to enhance our curriculum and programs. I encourage all of my translation and interpretation students to take CAT and Localization Management classes even if they do not plan to pursue a career in localization. They need to learn how to work with tools and with translation and localization managers.

The Guide to Translation and Localization

Zac Westbrook

Tsőm élpőép llíw éčñâlg ťâ síhť dñâ píks ťhgír ťsâp tí. Kőől â éltťíl résőlč, hgüőhť, dñâ ll'üőy éés üőy ñâč dñâťsrédñü tí őñ mélbőrp! Sâ â sčíťsíügñíl rőjâm, I tñéps srüőh ñőpü srüőh ñí égéllőč gñírâťs ťâ ñgíérőf txéť gñíyrt őt réhpíčéd émős ñréťťâp rő réhťőñâ dñâ ékâm ésñés fő tí ñévé fí I révéñ déñrâél éhť égâügñâl. Ehť sllíks I dépőlévéd gñíőd ťâhť érâ ylbídérčñí ydñâh sâ â Nőíťâzílâčől MP, dñâ I lééf ylbídérčñí ykčül őt yllâüťčâ őd gñíhťémős rőf â gñívíl ťâhť séťâlér őt ym séídüťs dñâ ym ñőíssésbő hťíw égâügñâl.

Why don't you try your hand at it? No decoder ring required.

Simplifying Project Management

Ok, so your files are uploaded, traceable, and secure. Now what? As we've discussed, not all content is going to be handled the same way. The gains you achieved by automating how projects are dispatched can easily be lost if everything thereafter is performed manually. Whether your vendor receives your files via email or a translation portal, their next step will likely be to have a project manager examine what you sent. The project manager will interpret your instructions, set up the appropriate workflow with the right tasks in the right order, and then assemble a team to execute the plan they've made. For instance, a project manager will (in accordance with existing agreements between you and your vendor) decide how many translation steps would be most appropriate for that particular project, and which additional services, such as formatting or QA, are needed and to what degree.

If your projects tend to be infrequent or it's necessary to generate a quote and obtain approval for each one, a full-fledged TMS might be overkill. On the other hand, if you're constantly submitting pre-approved projects that are similar in nature, a TMS may be able to shorten timelines and reduce costs by using workflow templates.

Rather than relying on a project manager to repetitively create each new project from scratch, a TMS may even be able to determine the appropriate workflow at the time of submission (based on pre-defined criteria) and then automatically assign the appropriate personnel to each task.

The specialists who are assigned to each pending task can then go directly to the TMS portal to retrieve any files along with the instructions needed to complete the work. Depending on the workflow, they can then perform their task(s) directly within the TMS, or download the files to work on locally before uploading their output back into the TMS. As each task is completed, the next person in line is automatically notified that it's their turn. Nobody has to wait for the project manager to notify them or wait for the project manager to send files. Compared to a "manual" method of processing translation work, a TMS offers a significant advantage in that it keeps the project moving without constant intervention from a project manager.

Integrating your TMS with CAT tools may yield even more efficiencies. For example, depending on which system you select, your linguists may be able to consolidate the various tools they're using anyway (translation memories, MT tools, termbases, etc.), or maybe even work on translations directly within the TMS itself. Likewise, a TMS might also support file treatment tasks by incorporating technologies typically used by engineers to convert files from their original type into the specialized formats used by translators. How much work can actually be performed within a TMS depends on the sophistication of the software and its integration with other tools.

Translation Management Systems

SOLD! ... to the Lowest Bidder

Who doesn't love a good auction? Some of the more sophisticated TMSs offer what is known as a "Vendor Marketplace." In its most extreme use, a vendor marketplace allows companies to put every job out for bid so that they can try to obtain the lowest price possible. In other cases, the functionality is used to house the contracted pricing from the LSPs whom they've selected as approved vendors. Then, when projects come up, the requestor can either select the vendor they want to use, or they can initiate an auction. If the latter, the vendors who are invited to participate will be provided with access to the files, a description of the requested services, any other necessary information, and a request to submit their lowest and best offer.

Obtaining the best deal is always exciting, but experienced translation buyers will caution that when quality matters, there are significant advantages to using the same team of translators from one project to the next. If you think about the books you read from your favorite authors or the memos you get from your colleagues at work, everyone writes with a unique style. The same concept applies to translators. Furthermore, over time, dedicated linguistic teams become familiar with your content as well as your stylistic and linguistic preferences. So if consistency from one project to the next is important to your end users, you won't get it by conducting an auction and shopping every project.

Using a TMS does not mean you have to go auction, nor does it mean you won't be able to continue using your favorite vendor. But you will want to understand the functionality and pick the features that are right for your company's localization needs.

"Connectors"

Although making project management more efficient is a mainstay of most TMSs, many are able to further streamline production by integrating other technologies.

Traditionally, the term "connector" referred to a piece of software that linked your CMS with a TMS, and possibly your CAT tools as well, to reduce the number of handoffs and simplify project starts. Any new or updated content produced by your CMS would be automatically dispatched for translation as soon as it was ready. Then, once that content had been localized, the translated deliverable was automatically returned and uploaded back into your database so that it was available for publishing.

Today, however, this term may also refer to a highly specialized interface that was developed specifically to enable users to receive and easily work with the output from other specialized content creation applications like Marketo, Adobe, Magento, Demandware, Drupal, and WordPress. These new "connectors" may or may not integrate with your TMS, but they will output "prepped" files that can be imported into most CAT tools. If your translation vendor does not have the engineering chops to work with the files that are output from these systems, then connectors such as these are a must.

Michael Phoenix

I was born at a very early age and throughout my work life have gotten to interact with both computer nerds like myself and normal people. I love working at LanguageLine because it is the only place that I have ever been employed where my coworkers are almost as weird as me. If you think I'm kidding, read some of the other bios. Still, it has been decided that it is best for me to work remotely at home under adult supervision and away from any sharp objects. Kind of like the way some families used to keep their crazy uncle locked downstairs in the root cellar.

ASK AN EXPERT:

How will new technologies reshape the role of human translators?

Florian Faes, Slator Co-Founder

Technologies such as adaptive machine translation and machine translation powered by neural networks are set to dramatically increase the productivity of human translators. In the coming decade (beyond that, who knows) human translators will interact much more closely with systems that are actually useful in accelerating translation speed and helping maintain quality.

Even if your vendor's engineers can work with these file types, there may be efficiencies from automating as many of the engineering tasks as possible. On the other hand, some of these connectors can carry a steep cost that's easily avoided by selecting an LSP who has the engineering skills to work with most any file type.

This is another reason to be sure to ask lots of questions about capabilities when picking a translation partner. One of the primary reasons that these connectors exist in the first place is that only a limited number of LSPs actually employ localization engineers … or if they do, engineers who can work with the output from the newest design applications. Without them, they simply can't handle your project.

Be Careful Out There

To provide the various services a TMS can encompass, many of the largest LSPs in the industry have developed proprietary software tools (SAAS, homegrown, or even open source). Be careful, though! Many companies say they have a TMS, but as you can see from this chapter, "having a TMS" can mean a lot of things. There is no single feature that defines a TMS, and as the name suggests, it's really more of a concept—a system—than a discrete object. Some TMSs may do nothing more than make submitting files a little easier, while others might be completely integrated, end-to-end systems that essentially automate the translation process.

Either way, the primary function of a TMS is to serve as a gateway to your translation resources. Despite some vendors' lofty aspirations for complete and total automation, there are still human beings behind the curtain performing the most essential tasks in the workflow. In other words, while technology can reduce the amount of work that LSPs need to perform, a successful localization program is still dependent on humans.

In summary, it is important to focus on what you want to achieve with a TMS rather than simply selecting the system with the most bells and whistles. Make sure you understand what you vendor's TMS solution can and cannot do with respect to your localization needs and your existing processes. It's entirely possible that a TMS is *not* right for you, especially given the costs that can be associated with these systems.

In an effort to recover development costs, some vendors try to indiscriminately put all of their customers in the TMS box, but this solution should really be reserved for clients with specific needs like those discussed in this chapter. Even if your vendor offers to provide TMS services free of charge, don't be lured in by what seems to be a smoking deal. Always test the quality of the output rather than the design of the TMS interface.

Chapter 17

Localizing Web Content With a Translation Proxy

by Kevin Cohn – SVP of Operations at Smartling

Kevin Cohn

Your translation providers have been selected, your contracts have been signed, and your team is excited to finally see their localization strategy come to life. Now, how will you pass text back and forth between your web properties and your translators?

That deceptively simple question is often the source of immense frustration.

The text you seek to translate must first be extracted from the website or web application it lives within. If the underlying software code has not been previously configured to support multilingual content, developers must manually sort through the code and isolate the requested text strings. This process of internationalization takes months—and possibly years— to complete as IT teams address this labor-intensive work alongside their everyday responsibilities.

Project managers then typically paste the captured source text into a spreadsheet and email it to the assigned translator. Or, more sophisticated teams might upload strings directly to a shared translation management system (TMS). Once completed translations pass quality assurance protocols and are approved for publication, website developers or application administrators must find time on their calendars to upload the target text.

It doesn't take a Six Sigma Certification to spot the inefficiencies here. And the problems only get worse as corporate content sprawls across more systems and into more languages.

As SVP of Operations at Smartling, Kevin oversees the professional services, technical support, customer success, and business operations teams of a localization industry leader. Prior to joining Smartling, Kevin served as COO at Atypon, a web and mobile content delivery and monetization platform.

What A Translation Proxy Is Designed To Do

Automating the delivery of web content to and from translation environments is the only way to execute localization strategies with modern efficiency and serious scale. A translation proxy is simply the high-speed track over which that content travels.

This innovative solution eliminates the need to internationalize code before text can be extracted from a website or content management system (CMS). The translation proxy automatically pulls strings from the presentation layer of a page, instead of inspecting the code base of every supporting system. As a result, project managers can quickly gather the desired source text without any IT assistance and immediately initiate the associated translation workflows.

The content publishing process can be addressed independently as well. Instead of deferring to website developers and application administrators, the proxy takes on the task of updating pages with completed translations. When web users make a request for localized content, the proxy quickly swaps out source text for target text and delivers the desired page in a matter of milliseconds.

ASK AN EXPERT:

How will new technologies reshape the role of human translators?

Jack Welde, Smartling

Co-Founder & CEO

Companies will blend machine and human resources more aggressively — and that's good news for all involved. Specialized content, such as marketing, legal, and pharma, will still be best performed by professional, human translators. But technology will be selectively employed to address the tedious tasks that distract translators from applying their true professional talents. At a higher level, adaptive machine translation, predictive text tools, and smarter contextual solutions will help translators process content faster while proactively reducing errors.

How A Translation Proxy Operates

Translation proxy servers sit between web users and source websites, responding only to requests for localized web pages. Assuming your source website is published in English, user requests for original English web pages will bypass the proxy entirely and go directly to your hosting environment. As a result, it must be acknowledged that the translation proxy has no impact whatsoever on source website traffic.

To provide a localized website experience for French users, all you would need to do from an IT perspective is make a one-time configuration change that points your French domain (fr.yourcompany.com) to your proxy provider's servers. From that point forward, traffic to this localized website would be handled with the following protocol:

- Localized web page request goes directly to proxy server
- Proxy captures a snapshot of the source web page by calling your servers
- This snapshot is parsed to identify each source text string
- Proxy swaps completed translations in for corresponding source text
- The resulting French web page is delivered directly to the user

This approach does not delay or disrupt the user experience in any material way, and has delivered reliable results for companies of every size and sector. But as we will discuss, there are several business scenarios where adopting a translation proxy is particularly advantageous.

Use Case #1 – Accelerating Time to Market

Some companies see localized sites as a luxury they'd like to explore in another year or two. Other organizations regard localized sites as burning business priorities that need to go live next month. When you relate more with the latter group, a translation proxy is almost always the answer.

If your web properties are not already configured to support multilingual content, your odds of an expedited launch are already in danger. It could be months before you're able to deploy the developers required to tackle code internationalization and capture source content. And even if that engineering work were previously addressed, copying and pasting text strings into spreadsheets would still create a considerable lag.

The only realistic way of hitting aggressive deadlines is to reject these manual tasks entirely and leverage a proxy solution that immediately places source text in your translators' hands.

The value of this speed cannot be understated. For an eCommerce retailer, launching localized sites ahead of the holiday shopping season could be the difference between missing annual revenue projections and beating the board's expectations. For a luxury hotel chain, localizing this quarter could be the difference between competing in an emerging market and capturing the dominant share of it. For WeWork, it meant quickly complying with multilingual regulations when the coworking innovator was first expanding its operations to Quebec.

Use Case #2 – Solving Content Sprawl

The days of filtering all corporate content through a single webmaster are already a distant memory for most companies. The text that populates modern web pages now originates from a wide array of content management platforms operated by an ever-expanding cast of contributors. For global travel giant British Airways, a myriad of discrete web services underlie the company's online booking engines alone.

This evolution has primarily been a positive development. Business teams have exponentially increased the speed and scale of their content strategies while technical teams have happily retreated from the role of gatekeeper. But the continued sprawl of corporate content does pose problems when it comes time to localize.

Manually gathering and replacing text from every content repository, marketing automation platform, and eCommerce enablement tool owned by the organization will strain the interdepartmental collaboration skills of any project manager. Even if they can complete the mission, some of that source content will likely be updated by the time everything gets packaged, translated, and approved anyway. As a result, your localized content may never quite match the latest version of its source site.

In theory, business teams could improve efficiency by working exclusively with localization-ready systems or tasking developers with engineering a fix for any tool that isn't. But in reality, those strategies are impractical at best and impossible at worst.

A translation proxy helps companies sidestep all of these unfortunate scenarios by parsing web content from the presentation layer of the page. As a result, content creators can continue working in their systems of choice while the proxy continuously captures their updates and automatically carries that text into the translation environment. All a project manager has to do is decide which strings they'd like translators to process first.

At the same time, IT teams can take heart knowing that translation technology won't weigh down their core infrastructure. A proxy sits apart from the source website and only becomes an active player when called upon to deliver its specialized services. It's a continuously available resource that doesn't demand maintenance from the IT team or necessitate significant changes to complementary network components.

Use Case #3 – Minimizing Opportunity Costs

The previous two use cases imply that, to a certain extent, the decision to adopt a translation proxy is a consequence of a company's limitations. Deadlines are too near, systems are too complex, and IT teams are too swamped to save the day. These are all deeply felt scenarios, to be sure, but they don't resonate with every organization.

There are plenty of businesses that believe they have all the resources they need to execute the localization strategy they want. Budgets are sufficient, staff are available, and deadlines are negotiable. In these scenarios, though, opportunity cost is the hidden variable so few consider.

How localization teams consume IT resources can quickly become a company-wide concern in an era when "software is eating the world." Technical talent is precious, and it's in the best interest of your business to keep developers engaged in innovative tasks that demand their most dynamic skills. Manually internationalizing code and uploading web content fit neither description.

Building an API-based solution that replicates certain translation proxy features may feel more proactive, but tech-savvy companies should still take time to assess how such a project could impact competing priorities. Will the hours spent supporting localization disrupt product roadmaps and delay delivery of more impactful assets?

In the case of home security solution provider Canary, localization administrators immediately acknowledged the business value of maintaining the company's rapid product release schedule and decided to leverage a translation proxy to resolve their own technical requirements.

Software developers aren't the only translation teammates whose time holds value, either. How many more languages could project managers oversee if their days weren't defined by spreadsheets? How ambitious might marketers become if they knew localized content could be updated in days instead of weeks? These are the kind of outcomes every company needs to consider when deciding which translation technologies to employ.

Caveats & Considerations

A translation proxy is ultimately nothing more than a new expression of an old method. Proxy servers have been around since the dawn of network computing and continue to improve user experiences all across the modern web. They accelerate page loads, facilitate secure logins, and keep objectionable content off corporate networks.

I feel the need to reiterate these basic principles because translation proxies have mysteriously become a magnet for irrational fear and misplaced blame.

Any concerns regarding the security, hosting, and performance of source websites can quickly be resolved by recognizing that a translation proxy operates independently of your website in the same way that any common content delivery network would.

When it comes to localized websites, international SEO concerns can be alleviated as well. A translation proxy is only intended as a means of transforming a content experience for multiple locales—it is not responsible for formulating the content strategy behind it. Regardless of how localized sites are created, companies eager to capture search traffic need to diligently incorporate the on-page optimization strategies recommended by SEO experts with local market knowledge.

Again, a translation proxy is merely the expression of a method. Some vendors express it more elegantly and efficiently than others, but none can claim it as a comprehensive localization solution. Only by pairing the proxy with a suitable TMS can you start to appreciate the full value of optimized content collection, translation, and distribution.

About Smartling
Smartling's enterprise translation management platform helps brands gain a more competitive global position by transforming the way their content is created and consumed around the world. Smartling's technology helps brands access new markets, more customers, and greater value. The company is headquartered in NYC with more than 150 employees spread across its 5 global offices. For more information, please visit www.smartling.com.

CHAPTER 18

Content Management Systems
(The "Secret Sauce" for Dramatically Reducing your Localization Costs)

It is not uncommon for some customers to have a bit of sticker shock when they receive their first quote for translation. Translation and localization can be expensive. For example, the cost of a relatively straightforward project can easily be $10,000 or even $100,000 depending on how many words and how many languages you need to translate. What most people don't realize, however, is that a high quality translation requires a large team of skilled professionals.

When compared to other professional services, it is easy to see that localization is actually quite the bargain, especially in comparison to the $150 per hour your CPA charges or the $250 per hour you spend for your attorney. Typically, translation buyers only end up paying about $30 to $40 per hour for work that is performed by highly trained professionals with advanced degrees and many years of experience. Moreover, the essential services these specialists provide have an immensely positive impact on the quality of the product you end up with and its ultimate acceptance in the marketplace. Put another way, they are well worth the money!

Nevertheless, understanding why translation services are expensive doesn't change the practical reality that many companies have limited resources to spend on them. And so it's no surprise that some buyers search high and low for ways to save a few dollars. For many this means shopping projects from one vendor to another. As tempting as it may be to try this, beware the consequences! Using the same vendor from one job to the next almost always yields higher quality deliverables, so long as they assign the same translators to each project. Be sure to ask! As the linguists become familiar with your stylistic and terminology preferences, the resulting translations will become more consistent.

Likewise, negotiating for a one or two cent reduction in the price you pay per word is equally short sighted and ineffective. Even if you're able to bring your vendor down from say $0.26 to $0.25 per word for a German translation, for example, the net savings is probably going to be disappointing. You would have to translate a million words to realize just $10,000 in savings. More significantly, it could result in your vendor using underqualified translators or simply omitting important steps from their workflow to compensate for the lost revenue, which will invariably leave you with an inferior product.

Even a DIY approach won't have a huge impact once you factor in the costs and time associated with everything that entails: identifying and recruiting the resources you will need, independently contracting each person and negotiating rates, coordinating the execution of each project, and troubleshooting every hiccup along the way. Just because you're not paying a vendor to do these things doesn't mean they're free to you, and if anyone could do them with same aplomb as a professional, the Language Services market would not exist.

In the end, no matter how good your negotiating skills are, the "tweaks" that language service professionals can make to their quotes by adjusting their per word rates by a couple of pennies or modifying their workflow rarely exceed 10 percent, and are usually less than 5 percent. And while you should always be a savvy shopper, keep in mind that if one vendor's quote is significantly less than another's, more often than not it is because they are not proposing the same services. As described more fully in Chapter 5, it is pretty certain that the cheaper one is going to (a) use less qualified translators, (b) perform fewer quality assurance steps, or (c) both. Are the minimal savings worth a lower quality deliverable?

The Guide to Translation and Localization

Sarah LaRue

If your Nerve, deny you—
Go above your Nerve—
Emily Dickinson

Also, "Life is either a daring adventure or nothing."
Helen Keller

Also, "If it scares you, it might be a good thing to try." *Seth Godin*

Living my life one mountain, ocean, river, forest and desert at a time … Eventually, I will walk across the entire surface of the planet. But for now, Oregon has enough beautiful natural spaces to at least quench some of my wanderlust.

"Go climb that godd**n mountain."
Jack Kerouac

Content Management to the Rescue

There is one option available to customers who want to dramatically reduce their localization costs, but you must be willing to completely change how you create and then publish the content that gets localized to achieve it.

As illustrated in the diagram below, localization is usually treated as a silo unto itself, and all efforts to save a few dollars take place within the confines of that silo. In reality, however, localization is just one part of a broader workflow that includes important elements both before and after it. First, the content that is going to be translated has to be created. This is typically done by professional writers in a "tech pubs" department who use MS Word, InDesign, or any number of other creative applications. Then, after the materials have been translated, the localized versions have to be published to either print or digital formats, or both.

By implementing a content management system (CMS) to integrate localization with what happens before (specifically, creating the materials in the first place) along with what happens after (i.e., publishing the translated versions), companies can often save 50 to 60 percent on localization!

Benefits of a CMS

The primary benefit of a CMS is that it separates your written content from any particular document, file, or format, and makes that content easier to manage. Here's a common example to illustrate this concept:

Let's say that every month you make updates to a newsletter that is distributed as a printable PDF and is also available on your company website. Typically this means that you'll need to have your writer update the copy, your graphic designer make any changes to your design files in one place, and then your webmaster will have to update your HTML files with the same changes in another place.

But wouldn't it be great if you could modify and update that common text in just one place and then automatically disseminate the newsletter everywhere with just the push of a button? A CMS can allow you to do just that. It gives you the ability to manage all of your written content in one place and then simultaneously publish multiple versions in any format from a single source.

Not only that, but as you produce more and more content, a CMS stores it in small, reusable components (anything from a word to a paragraph), which are often referred to as "chunks." Whether you need to update existing content, or create original material for a new publication, a CMS makes all of your "legacy" text available to you and allows you to change it, add to it, and re-combine it however you see fit. This not only promotes the re-use of content, but also eliminates the need to clumsily copy text from one file to another in order to re-use it. Not surprisingly, this can yield significant cost savings before localization is ever considered, and shortens the time needed to produce both new and updated publications.

Manual Writing vs. a Structured CMS

Moving to a CMS requires significant changes to your writing and publication process. Not only does using a CMS mean that content is developed independently from the publishing process, but also that the content being written might be used in more than one place and in more than one medium.

In addition to changing how you view the process of producing and managing content for future use, however, your writing team may need to reconsider how they're writing your content in the first place. Because content is traditionally produced document by document, writers are often concerned with the cohesiveness and flow of the text within just that document. As such, they may focus on how the text flows and how different sections relate to each other in that particular context. Since a CMS is designed to efficiently re-use content, your writers will need to start considering how they can produce independent "chunks" of content that can be seamlessly recombined. This means standardizing the characteristics of your content so that your final publications don't resemble a Rube Goldberg contraption after several disparate pieces are assembled into one.

A good analogy for this process is the evolution of automotive manufacturing. Before Henry Ford, each car was essentially hand built from individual parts. Workers started with a bare chassis, and put together the car part by part until it was finished and driven away. Although very similar to each other, each car was likely to have its own idiosyncrasies. As manufacturing techniques evolved, fabrication shifted from individual parts to major assemblies produced all over the world. Today, most cars, even the traditionally hand-built models, are constructed from dozens of pre-manufactured components resourced worldwide. Most significantly, vehicle frames are often used in more than one model, and even brand, of car.

Structured writing is a similar concept; contributors all produce content that is akin to an automotive assembly line. At the time of publication, the appropriate content is collected into a final product that is then plugged into a template to be presented in whatever fashion is desired.

Integrating the Localization Process

In the preceding paragraphs, we described how a CMS makes it more efficient to produce and manage your source content. But how can the features of a CMS be integrated with your localization workflow to save you money? First, if you're publishing from a CMS, you will no longer need to send both your InDesign (INDD) *and* HTML files, for example, to your translation vendor to create localized copies of each. This will reduce the time and costs associated with file preparation (localization engineering) and translating repeated text, but that's just the beginning.

As mentioned already, localization is often treated as a stand-alone silo, disconnected and independent from what happens before and after content is translated. But a localization-friendly CMS can erode the barriers between translation and the rest of your workflow, allowing content creation, localization, and publishing to happen in concert. Let's look first at how a CMS revamps things that traditionally happen *before* localization.

ASK AN EXPERT:

What do you think will be the next largest area of growth in this industry?

Dr. Nitish Singh (Ph.D. MBA, MA), Brand2Global Program Leader (Global Digital Marketing & Localization Certification)

For the Localization & Translation industry the next growth phase will not be regarding competing based on cost per word, but competing based on rare and inimitable capabilities related to localizing various aspects of global marketing. Capabilities related to localizing brand assets, localizing social media assets, localizing overall global marketing strategy. Also, capabilities related to international marketing research on locale-specific consumer preferences, cultural customization of various digital interfaces and digital content, and technologies that enhance localization tool and process efficiencies.

The Guide to Translation and Localization

Natalya Agayev

In my spare time I enjoy reading a good novel. Sometimes I even venture to the poetry section—from the 19th century, good ol' Golden Age of Russian Poetry. A favorite excerpt written by Alexander Pushkin:

*Я помню чудное мгновенье:
Передо мной явилась ты,
Как мимолетное виденье,
Как гений чистой красоты.*

Many CMS applications employ an "authoring memory" that makes previously created source content available for re-use. But the best CMSs will also tell you which portions of your existing content have already been translated and into which languages. You can imagine how useful this is for authors and their managers. With this information at their fingertips, writers who know that the document they are working on will eventually be localized simply pick the version that has already been translated. In other words, why write a completely new passage of text and submit it for translation, if you know that an equivalent passage has already been translated into multiple languages?

If you have read Chapter 15 of this book, you may be asking why this matters. After all, doesn't a translation memory identify any text that has been previously translated so that it can be reused? The answer is that yes it does; but content created from a CMS will invariably yield even more leveraging because authors are more likely to select passages that have already been translated when presented with a choice. Not only does this mean that you control the exact number of words your vendor will need to translate, but with a properly integrated CMS it's entirely possible that for some projects you'll find that you need no translation at all—because all the text you need for any language is already available in your database and perfectly organized for you to re-use as needed.

The second and usually more significant way that a CMS reduces localization costs is by using pre-configured templates to facilitate publication of the translated materials (i.e. by integrating the localization silo with what happens *after* translation). These templates are based on the design specifications of your webpage, marketing collateral or manuals and, if constructed well, won't need to be formatted by DTP specialists.

Contrast this with how content is customarily published whereby highly skilled professional formatters spend countless hours ensuring that the translated versions are just as perfect as the original source documents, and it's easy to understand how CMS generated templates can dramatically reduce the cost of localizing. Instead of relying on your designers to take the copy from your technical writers and turn it into INDD and HTML files (and then on their counterparts at your language services vendor to create localized copies of these files), you can instead publish all versions of your files in all languages with the push of a few buttons. And, since these templates are assembling the components of the resulting output with technological precision, not only is there no need for humans to format them, there is no need to QA them for human formatting errors either. The resulting savings can be as much as 30 percent to 40 percent of the total project cost.

In addition to all of the above, CMS applications have other simple features to streamline translation and localization. Even though your QA needs might be reduced through the use of a CMS, your localized content should always be proofread once it's laid out in context. If you're constantly updating large manuals however, it can easily become costly or time prohibitive to have a professional linguist re-read the entire manual each time. Luckily, CMSs can allow you to identify or isolate (within your published file) what content is new and/or updated. Now, just like your content authors, the proofreader can ignore your tried and true legacy content, focusing only on what's new or unique to a publication or product.

Is a CMS Worth the Trouble?

To be sure, implementing a CMS is not for everyone. For many organizations it means completely changing how they create and publish content. And, depending on which application you purchase, it can be expensive. As you contemplate whether a CMS is the right solution for your business, there are several questions to consider:

- Frequency of translations: Is it likely that you will translate your source content?
- Quantity of content produced: Do your technical writers create and maintain tens, hundreds, or thousands of pages of documentation?
- Frequency of updates: Once content is translated, is it subject to change on a frequent basis, or does it remain stable?
- Number of target languages: Do you translate into more than one target language and, if so, is all content translated into all languages or is some content translated into some languages but not others?
- Published outputs desired: Do you publish the same content in multiple formats (e.g., a spec sheet for print, web, and specification summaries)?

If you answered "yes" to any of these questions, it probably makes sense to investigate whether a CMS is right for your company. But even if you're not a large user of language services, the efficiencies and other benefits that you can achieve when creating source content may still be worth your effort. As you evaluate the business case for implementing a CMS, keep in mind that not all CMS tools, or even strategies, are the same.

Which tool is appropriate for you will depend on the following factors:

- The structure of the teams producing your written content;
- Your content creation, editing and approval process;
- Your publication process;
- How your existing English and localized content will be migrated from their current formats into a CMS (importing legacy content and setting up publishing templates can be a major undertaking); and
- The impact it will have on your employees who will likely see the nature of their responsibilities change, including technical writers and other content contributors, webmasters, marketing managers, IT staff, localization managers, and translation vendors.

The best localization vendors will not only be familiar with CMS tools, but will be an invaluable partner as you transition to a CMS-based workflow. By ensuring that all of the localization related steps are fully streamlined and integrated, they will help you maximize the savings that result therefrom.

ASK AN EXPERT:

What do you think will be the next largest area of growth in this industry?

Laura Brandon, GALA Executive Director

Two key areas come to mind when considering the growth of the industry: machine translation integration services and remote interpreting services. More and more companies are adopting machine translation in parts of their workflow, promising growth for the companies that can guide and support MT set-up. Meanwhile, there is a lot of buzz in the interpreting technology arena related to various voice technologies. Interesting new solutions are challenging old models, making interpreting services more accessible and affordable than in the past.

ASK AN EXPERT:

What does language access mean now to your organization? In 5 years?

Salvatore "Salvo" Giammarresi, PayPal Head of Content & Globalization

PayPal's global vision is to give people better ways to manage and move their money and offering them choice and flexibility in how they are able to send money, pay or get paid. Language access fully supports our vision. In five years, I expect PayPal to offer an even wider language footprint.

ROI of a CMS

Over the years, there are two observations that the LanguageLine team has noted whenever one of our customers has implemented a CMS:

Their localization costs decrease by 40 to 60 percent, and

Their total localization spending actually goes up.

At first blush, spending more on localization may seem counterintuitive, and not the goal you had in mind. The reality though is almost every organization would like to translate more content than they do. So if you can significantly reduce the cost to translate, the resulting return on your investment in localization will increase dramatically, often to the point where the financial return is such that it now makes sense to translate material that previously would have been left untranslated.

In general, it is advisable to define ROI over a 6-month, 12-month, or 18-month horizon, and evaluate the payoff in both dollars and production time. If you have a consistent basis for comparison, calculating the ROI of your localization spending is a simple matter. It is even easier if you have your prospective localization vendor do the calculations for you. The CMS tool vendors may also be able to generate an ROI calculation, but it is best to have a custom calculation developed based on your particular business situation.

At LanguageLine, we always recommend that you run a pilot project to confirm the savings and test the effectiveness of a CMS. If you take this route, begin by translating a project using a traditional workflow to establish base measurements for time and cost. You also will want to get an idea of just how much you can leverage your existing translation memories against the new content format, as you may lose some leveraging between your traditional file formats and the CMS content as a result of conversion issues.

Fortunately, a vendor with an expert engineering staff can help make your experience with integrating localization and your CMS easy and less expensive. Note, however, that the biggest savings will result from complete integration of your CMS with both your own business systems and your localization vendor's translation management system. For this reason it is difficult to overstate how important it is to select the right vendor.

Next, you will want to execute the same project using the CMS. Since you will likely be running an evaluation copy of the software and may not have imported all of your existing content or created fully polished templates, the resulting savings will be less than what you will achieve a few months down the road, but should be sufficient to determine if a CMS makes sense for your organization.

Chapter 19
Machine Translation

Commercial Machine Translation Solutions

In Chapter 3, we discussed how free tools such as Google Translate and Microsoft Skype are a quick and easy way to help people get a basic understanding of what something says, but also why you're probably not going to be too impressed if you try to use them to localize your technical manuals. In contrast, commercial MT applications, while still not a match for human translators alone, can be an effective part of a localization workflow for some materials in some situations.

To better understand the implications of machine translation for the translation and localization industry, and more importantly, for the consumers of these services, it's helpful to look at something totally unrelated: chess.

In 1996, Grand Champion Gary Kasparov lost a game of chess to the IBM computer Deep Blue—the first time in history that a human lost to a computer at chess. Soon after, technology reached a point where even teams of the world's brightest minds were no longer competitive in chess games against computers. For some, events like this signal what seems to be the foregone conclusion of so much science fiction: Machines are slowly taking over and will soon do everything humans can do and more.

And now that computers can also beat Jeopardy! champions and even compose original music, it makes sense to wonder why they can't translate better than humans too? Part of the answer lies in realizing that the humans-and-computers-as-adversaries trope is best left to fiction. In reality, humans and machines have forged and an incredibly powerful alliance. The advent of "Freestyle" chess, a variation where humans and computers team up to compete against other computers, neatly illustrates this point. As Kasparov himself noted, "The teams of human plus machine dominated even the strongest computers. The chess machine Hydra, which is a chess-specific supercomputer like Deep Blue, was no match for a strong human player using a relatively weak laptop. Human strategic guidance combined with the tactical acuity of a computer was overwhelming."

What we are witnessing with these astounding advances in technology is not humans losing some kind of war against the machine, but rather humans gaining incredible tools. The effect is perhaps more pronounced within the realm of language and translation simply because, unlike chess, effective communication also depends on inherent, abstract elements such as culture and emotion. While technology will undoubtedly continue to increase productivity, lower costs, and take over a lot of the "grunt work" involved in translation, human involvement will still be the "X factor" required to produce the best results possible.

To be sure, the topic of machine translation remains controversial in localization circles with some arguing that machine translation is and will remain a useless endeavor, while others argue that we're on the cusp of a breakthrough that will allow its potential to be fully realized. The truth is somewhere between these extremes. Below is a brief overview of how MT works, its history, how it is used already in the industry, and of course, where it falls short.

The Guide to Translation and Localization

Kurt Schneider

I work for a company that focuses on languages and words; yet I focus on numbers. When I was younger, I wanted to be a golf pro. In golf, the lower the number the better. In business, it's just the opposite; the bigger the number the better. My passions outside of work include playing golf, playing the guitar, volunteering at a pit bull rescue, and last but certainly not least, taking care of and spending time with my own two pit bulls, Presley and Priscilla (yes, I'm obsessed with Elvis!).

Rule Based, Statistical, and Neural Network MT

One of the earliest approaches to MT was rule based machine translation, which essentially involves "teaching" computers about specific languages. First, a computational linguist would have to hand-code the unique linguistic rules for all applicable languages into the software itself and then the users have to customize bilingual dictionaries. Next, using those hand-coded rules, the software deconstructs and interprets the source text (called parsing), maps the pieces to the bilingual dictionary, and reassembles everything according to the target language's grammar. As a crude example, the system might encounter the word "financed" in English and break its meaning down into at least 2 parts: the concept of something financial, tied to the stem "financ-," and the concept of an action happening in the past, tied to the suffix "-ed." It will then find the corresponding "stem" for the concept of finance in the bilingual dictionary followed by the pre-coded grammatical rules to build the past tense verb form of that word in the target language. Note that this method actively generates translations and does not simply sort through individually-stored translations for all of a word's variants, e.g. "finance," finances," "financed." Rule-based systems are both costly and time-consuming to maintain and even more so when you want to add new language pairs.

Later, statistical machine translation, which relies on statistical word association methods to extrapolate the relationships between similar words and phrases rather than hand-coded linguistic rules, emerged as the preferred technology. In basic terms, a statistical MT engine will analyze some text in language "A" and some text in language "B" that it already knows is equivalent, and then make connections between individual words and small phrases. That is, the engine is saying that wherever we see this word in language "A," we most often see that word in language "B," so it's probably the right translation. When a new sentence is submitted for translation, the engine builds the translated sentence one word at a time based on these statistical associations. The resulting quality of the machine translation, however, depends on the quality and consistency of the original translations it's associating. If the original translations are wrong, so too will the machine translations be wrong; if half the bilingual data comes from computer manuals where "back up" means make extra copies, and half the bilingual data comes from plumbing systems manuals where "back up" means accumulate behind an obstruction, the engine has no way to know which meaning is intended in your sentence unless it has been "trained" over time to improve context-dependent translations based on human feedback. Still, compared to rule based engines, adding new language pairs is relatively cheap and fast, and they do not require a team of expert linguists to maintain.

Most recently, neural network machine translation technology has stolen the spotlight. It is similar to statistical MT in that it also requires large sets of bilingual data to associate equivalent text in two languages, but rather than statistically associating individual words in that data, it can consider entire sentences as the input for translation and map those to equivalent sentences in another language. To handle new sentences, neural network engines use advanced computational techniques to make inferences based on similar text in known sentences. They also leverage state of the art machine learning technology to vastly improve the engine's ability to be trained automatically. Although this approach to MT is relatively new and has had its own share of growing pains, researchers have achieved much higher quality compared to traditional phrase-based MT. In fact, in late 2016, Google rolled out a neural network based platform for Google Translate and started running numerous language pairs through it, claiming it reduces errors by 55%-85% for some language pairs.

Neural network MT is clearly an important advancement in the ongoing development of machine translation technology. But many issues still remain, including the time and cost needed to build and train MT engines, protection of intellectual property, and, most significantly, the fact that the output still contains errors that humans would never make. Whether or not machine translation would work as part of your solution depends on several other aspects discussed below.

Post-editing

In most situations, what you get directly "out of the box" from MT will be inadequate and will need to be corrected or polished by a human translator. As defined in Wikipedia, "Post-editing involves the correction of machine translation output to ensure that it meets a level of quality negotiated in advance between the client and the post-editor." This is a critical concept to understand. Consumers who decide to purchase machine translation with human post-editing effectively have to make a decision as to how many errors they are willing to accept in their final deliverable.

Any machine translation can be just as good as human translation if the post-editor does enough polishing. Of course, the more you polish, the longer it takes and the more it costs. If the purpose of MT is to provide faster, cheaper translations, this creates a dilemma for vendors who offer MT solutions.

To keep the price of machine translation lower than human translation, language service providers (LSPs) must restrict the number of changes an editor can make. Every change equals more time on the clock, and editors are paid by the hour. The leading vendors of MT solutions have sophisticated tools that count how many edits a post-editor makes. This information is then uploaded to the post-editor's profile and oftentimes those who make too many changes are barred from future assignments. By definition, this also means that there is no expectation that the final deliverable will be error free. Instead the LSP's goal is to make the translation "good enough," which is an inherently subjective concept.

The above notwithstanding, if you're using a highly customized, top of the line MT engine and you have a little luck along the way, you may be able to generate near-human quality translations with minimal editing. Generally this is not the case, however, and at a certain point the cost and effort of post-editing can eclipse the cost and effort of human translation with virtually no upside to quality.

One final warning: Some companies don't disclose that they are using MT with post editing and try to pass it off as 100% human translation. You need to ask. It's not the same.

ASK AN EXPERT:

What do you think will be the next largest area of growth in this industry?

Salvatore "Salvo" Giammarresi, PayPal Head of Content & Globalization

The localization industry still suffers from a lack of recognition. Essentially our industry needs to mature. While other functions like engineering, product management and design are well defined, understood and valued, many localization practitioners and teams still need to explain their role, how they are truly adding value and how they are a revenue-generating function and not just a cost line item.

The Pros of Using MT

There are many situations for which machine translation is a great solution. For example, when you just need to know what something says, simple MT systems (e.g., Google Translate) allow any user to get a "gist" translation almost instantaneously. Similarly, although the scale is much different, the US military used MT to quickly comb through the millions of pages of information that was found in connection with deployments over the last decade to determine what was useful intel and what wasn't. Likewise, this approach is often employed by law firms that need to quickly and cheaply sort through massive amounts of foreign language discovery documents in order to decide how and where to focus more expensive, but more reliable, human translation resources later on.

There are many applications for businesses too. If you want to find out whether your software application will still work properly if it is translated into French, an MT generated "pseudo-translation" is a cheap way to find out. Not only will you be able to test some of the functionality, but it also often reveals things you overlooked or assumptions you made during development. For example, you might discover that your code breaks if certain keywords or placeholder variables are inadvertently translated, or that the character limits for certain fields are set too low. Alternatively, you might realize that your code or system architecture is not compatible with non-Roman character sets or other linguistic features absent from English. Using MT to identify and isolate these issues prior to translation can save you lots of headaches.

Perhaps the biggest benefit of MT, though, is its ability to help translators and LSPs keep up with the increasing demand for translation. As companies realize how many benefits there are to communicating with customers in their own language, they also find that the amount of content they want to translate far exceeds what they have the time and money to do. Fortunately, when the translations don't need to be perfect, MT makes it possible to translate what would otherwise not get done.

MT can also increase translator productivity. The industry standard for a human translator is approximately 2,200 words daily. In contrast, technical translators who leverage machine translation can increase their throughput to as many as 7,000 words a day. This is not an estimate but actual data. Even on the low side, an increase to 4,400 words doubles a translator's daily output.

With the right controls in place and for the right type of content, MT can allow organizations to "do more with less." Do not, however, make the mistake of leaving professional translators out of the equation. Results always will be better with a human involved.

The Cons of Using MT

It's pretty hard to find anything that most people agree on, but MT quality may be one of them. Unless you're an MT geek, almost everyone would agree that pure MT output is not as good as human translation. As Nicholas Hartmann, former president of the American Translators Association put it, "There is a significant difference between what MTers and translators define as acceptable translation 'quality' in terms of accuracy, word choice, syntax, and general linguistic fidelity." In other words, machine translation technologists and professional linguists don't necessarily share the same goal when it comes to translation.

From a theoretical standpoint, the limitations of MT are also evident. Understanding messages in natural language sometimes relies on information which is not present in the words that make up a particular message. The Bar-Hillel paradox, provided by linguist Yehoshua Bar-Hillel as evidence that MT was impossible, is a classic example:

> The pen is in the box.
> [i.e. the writing instrument is in the container]

> The box is in the pen.
> [i.e. the container is in the playpen or the pigpen]

Taken at face value, it could be difficult even for a human to correctly infer the meaning of these sentences. It is not impossible of course, because we have direct access to a wealth of other information not present in either sentence. Our knowledge about all meanings of "pen" and "box," including their typical sizes, for example, allows us to confidently guess which meaning of each is intended in each sentence. It is even easier to determine which meanings are intended if there is a context preceding these sentences. Additional information about the context is carried over from one sentence to the next, but not present when the sentences are taken alone. There is an entire branch of linguistics, called discourse analysis, devoted to the study of how context affects the meaning of words and sentences. In order to correctly infer the meaning of ambiguous sentences like this, computers have to learn how to "remember" a context and make use of it to interpret the correct meaning of words and sentences within that context.

Depending on your perspective, another drawback of MT is that in order to maximize its effectiveness, input has to be tightly controlled. MT systems perform much better when simple and predictable syntax and semantics are used. But achieving this kind of regularity across all your source content before translation often requires training writers to produce language optimized for machine translation. Without a team of highly trained writers, most companies will find it very difficult to create MT-friendly content. Moreover, materials that contain abbreviations, slang, misspellings, misused or non-existent punctuation, or fragments will throw an MT engine for a loop. While variable word order, the presence of passive and active voice, irregular or ambiguous language, cultural references, word play, and double-entendres are all examples of things that are difficult, if not impossible, for any type of MT engine to handle correctly.

Conclusion

MT is an exciting technology that has great potential, but there is no one-size-fits-all approach, and purchasers of these services need to have a realistic expectation about what they will receive. In virtually no circumstances will the free and easily accessible tools such as Google Translate be adequate substitutes for a professional translator. And even those with greater capabilities will still require polishing by a human anyway. Thus, if you choose to go the MT route, the most important decision is not whether to use MT in the first place, but how much post-editing are you willing to pay for? Or, to say it another way, how many errors are you willing to accept?

There is certainly no doubt that MT has made incredible strides since it was first developed in the 1950s, and the latest systems allow users to accomplish translation tasks in less time for less money. However, despite more than six decades of research, MT has significant limitations, and if freestyle chess is any indication, output from even the best computer systems in the world will pale in comparison to what's possible when you keep humans in the picture.

Pete Landers

My fascination with languages began with singing. First there was church Latin and Bach in German, then came Italian and French opera. For singers, it is all about pronunciation and putting weight on significant words in order to convey the meaning. I didn't develop a big vocabulary by singing, but I did gain a big love for languages.

Later, when I was an assistant director in a literary arts center, I met some poets who created polyglot collage poems. Putting polyglot poetry into a little magazine turned out to be a lot of fun, and I began to immerse myself in knowledge of fonts and writing systems. Working at LanguageLine was a natural fit. During my time here I have had the pleasure of solving these font puzzles for languages I didn't even know existed. Even after many years I can be surprised by a previously unknown writing system.

Chapter 20

Over the Phone Interpretation

History of OPI Interpretation

Over the phone interpretation (OPI) began in San Jose, California in 1982. A rise in immigration and refugees due to conflicts in Southeast Asia came at the same time that a new telephone-based emergency reporting system was taking off in the US, 911. As these limited English proficient (LEP) individuals began using 911 to call for help or report a crime, the language barrier had an unprecedented impact on public safety. It was an old problem on a new scale. To remedy this issue, a San Jose police officer partnered with a US Marine interpreter to devise a volunteer-based telephone interpretation service. This enabled law enforcement personnel to connect to trained interpreters, so that they could communicate with the LEP community. From this, LanguageLine was born. We were the world's first OPI service.

Today it is estimated that the worldwide OPI market is a $1 billion industry that continues to grow every year, driven by global business expansion, new waves of immigration, and industry regulations that mandate improved language access.

How OPI Works

In its most basic form, OPI services are accessed by dialing a 1-800 number when users need to communicate with an interpreter. Typically, a live agent or a voice recognition system allows the user to specify the language they need, and seconds later, a professional interpreter of the requested language comes on the line. Some vendors accommodate the three-way call between you, the LEP, and the interpreter through specialty phones. These phones with two built-in handsets save call time and costs by eliminating the need to pass the phone back and forth.

Another option that eliminates the need to dial a 1-800 number, is to use a mobile application to access OPI services. This application allows for simple, one-touch access to the specific language required for interpretation. There is no need to remember a toll-free number. The user simply selects their language preference and the call is connected to the appropriate interpreter within seconds.

The app-based service is ideal for any number of situations where a language barrier impedes communication, whether it is an emergency or simply a business owner trying to facilitate a better experience for their customer. For example, when first responders meet an LEP in distress, they can use the mobile app to get ahold of a qualified interpreter quickly with just the touch of a button. These mobile apps are also ideal for individual consumers, allowing any casual user with a cell phone to gain access to an interpreter as well. A common example of this is a person traveling abroad on business. With a touch of a button, this person can gain access to an interpreter to successfully assist in brokering business deals with ease.

Over the Phone Interpretation

Technological Advancements

At LanguageLine, we have taken technology to the next level in innovation by developing a cloud-based platform that can handle the increased on-demand need for interpretation services. This type of infrastructure connects to multiple call centers and remote interpreters to support the hundreds of languages spoken today on a platform that is secure, reliable, and quickly scalable as the volume and complexity within the language access industry continues to grow. Partnering with a cloud-based language access vendor reduces your cost by eliminating the need for servers and other equipment and increases your revenue by making your services more accessible to your clients. This type of platform not only provides benefits to clients today, but is also the foundation for language access service innovation in the future.

Working with OPI Interpreters

Technology is only one part in finding the right vendor for your organization. The best language service providers will also offer quality testing and training as part of any language solutions package to ensure all interpreters are proficient in the call handling process. This process should prove their ability to express themselves grammatically, display a wide range of vocabulary, enunciate words, listen attentively, and use courteous language in both languages in order to ensure they apply proper phone protocols. Training should reinforce these abilities and cover the general rules on compliance, security and confidentiality. These lessons explain the specific regulations outlined within each policy, the implications of these rules, and how they are applied on each call.

ASK AN EXPERT:

What does quality mean?

Florian Faes, Slator Co-Founder

Describing quality in translation and interpretation is best addressed through a "I know it when I see it" approach. Whereas researchers and practitioners in machine translation look to quantify quality by using a so called BLEU score, applying a numerical value can only capture a few objective parameters without doing justice to the art that is translation and interpretation.

The Guide to Translation and Localization

ASK AN EXPERT:

Salvatore "Salvo" Giammarresi, PayPal Head of Content & Globalization

Quality means always putting the customer first—respecting and delighting the customer in every detail, in every interaction with your product and your company. When you think of quality in that way, then it becomes integral to everything you do and not an afterthought.

Providers should also have a plan in place to train employees on how to properly access these services and how to maximize the efficiency and effectiveness of the services. For example, interpreters are trained to repeat every word that is said. Therefore, if you are talking to an LEP named Jane and you say, "Please tell Jane to return to my office at 10:30 AM tomorrow," that is exactly what the interpreter will say. If, on the other hand, you say, "Return to my office at 10:30 AM tomorrow," your sentence will be much shorter and so will the interpreter's, without any change to your message. Your overall conversation length can be shortened by 20 percent or more when using direct speech like this, which not only allows you to cover more ground or have shorter meetings with LEP customers, but also reduces your cost proportionally.

Compliance and Regulatory Considerations

Decades ago, having a language access program that included services such as OPI was considered progressive and proactive; today it is required by law for many organizations. For instance, health care entities that receive federal funding from the US Department of Health and Human Services (HHS), HHS-administered programs, and Health Insurance Marketplaces are now required to comply with new federal language access requirements outlined in Section 1557 of the Affordable Care Act.

Other laws and regulations that your organization may need to comply with might include:

- Americans with Disabilities Act (ADA)
- Centers for Medicare & Medicaid Services (CMS)
- Executive Order 13166
- Equal Educational Opportunities Act (EEOA)
- Fraud, Waste and Abuse (FWA)
- Health Insurance Portability and Accountability Act (HIPAA)
- Protected Health Information (PHI)
- The Joint Commission
- Every Student Succeeds Act (Formerly No Child Left Behind)
- Title VI of the Civil Rights Act of 1964 (Title VI)

Do not let the number of laws and regulations intimidate you. They are straightforward and quite easy to understand. The regulations your organization are required to meet should be outlined as part of a needs assessment at the beginning of your search for a language access provider.

Best Questions to Ask When Choosing an LSP

So you want to hire an LSP, but you don't know where to start. By asking the questions below and comparing responses among potential vendors, you will be able to make an informed decision. For example, if accuracy is important, you will want to seek out a provider with a reputation for carefully screening, training and monitoring their telephonic interpreters. Another example would be if interpreters will have access to confidential information in their interactions with your clients. In this scenario, it is imperative that the LSP has appropriate security measures in place to protect this information. Smaller companies may not be able to provide sufficient security levels, reporting, or audit support. Likewise, some OPI companies may specialize in just a few uncommon languages, or a single language, such as Spanish, while others cover the whole gamut.

General
- How many interpreters do you have?
- How many languages do you offer?
- Can you provide a list of languages you offer and the times they are available?

Interpreter Proficiency, Training, and Monitoring
- How do you screen new interpreters and assess their proficiency?
- What level of proficiency do your interpreters need to have before they can start taking calls?
- Do your interpreters complete interpretation training?
- Can you describe the training they receive?
- Were your proficiency tests developed internally or externally validated? If external, what are their credentials?
- Do you provide training programs for specific industries?
- Do you have a monitoring program for your interpreters?
- What is the experience level of your monitors?

Reporting
- What reports will I receive?
- What information will be provided on these reports?
- Will the reports include connection times?

Security of Confidential Information
- Where are your interpreters located?
- What steps do you take to ensure the confidentiality of protected information?
- Are calls recorded?

Connection Times
- What is your average connection time for all languages?
- What is the average connection time for [my top language]?
- Are interpreters available 24/7 or just part of the day?
- What is the "up time" for your network?

The Guide to Translation and Localization

A leading French business newspaper is launching a multi-lingual version of its website using automatic translation, dispensing with journalists but producing often comic results.

"Ryanair loan to make travel of the passengers upright," read a typically bizarre headline on La Tribune's site this week above a story in equally mangled English on the low-cost airline's plans to make people fly standing up. "The Chinese car in ambush," "Internet Explorer: mistrust!" and "Assets of the continental right in management of the crisis" were some other mysterious headlines the same day on the site, which is still in an experimental phase.

Internal Considerations While Establishing OPI Service

In addition to investigating a prospective vendor's qualifications, it is also advisable to talk to colleagues in your organization to make sure you are choosing an LSP that meets everyone's needs. You will want to ask yourself:

Volume and Language Mix

- What is your annual average call volume?
- What languages have we needed historically?

Applications

- What departments will use the service?
- Do we need interpreters with specialized training (e.g., medical insurance, 911/emergency services)?
- How good does the service need to be?
- How important is accuracy?

Security, Audit Support and Reporting

- Do we need a provider that complies with HIPAA and HITECH laws?
- Do we need a provider that can support us with documentation during Joint Commission audits? (This applies to health care providers.)
- Do we require a dedicated account executive and ongoing training?
- Do we require reporting by language and minutes?

Top 5 Misconceptions about Phone Interpretation

New users of phone interpretation often have misconceptions about whether they really need the service or whether a cheaper approach will be good enough. Here are some of the common misconceptions:

Misconception: Why should I pay for this service? Can't I just find people who speak foreign languages and hire them on my own? Several of my employees speak another language. Can't I use them to interpret?

Correction: Interpreting is not the same as just speaking in two languages. This work requires a strong memory, excellent listening skills, extensive vocabulary, knowledge of standard protocols, and neutrality. A bilingual employee's skills are not comparable to a professional interpreter's skills.

Misconception: I only need a vendor who can support one, or two, or three languages.

Correction: You might think two or three languages is enough, but it's impossible to predict the languages your customers will speak. Using the right OPI vendor guarantees that you will be able to communicate with every one of your clients, no matter their location or country of origin. If you work in government, the languages you provide support for may be determined by local demographics, with the most common languages requiring interpretation and translation. But failure to provide interpretation to any LEP could result in fines.

It is best to have access to a large number of telephonic languages to prevent any misunderstandings or legal penalties.

Misconception:: I already use onsite interpreters so I do not need OPI.

Correction: When you need an interpreter quickly, an onsite interpreter is not a feasible option since they almost always need to be scheduled in advance. Even when they are already on premise, it still may take several minutes or more to walk from one building to the next inside a large hospital complex. In medical situations, a wait that long could be fatal.

Misconception: If immigrants speak some English, do they really need an interpreter?

Correction: A person who speaks "a little" or even "some" English is categorized as LEP and protected by laws ranging from Title VI of the Civil Rights Act of 1964 to Clinton Executive Order 13166.

Conclusion

Over the phone interpretation should be an important part of every organization's language access program. Not only is it available on demand whenever you need it, but it is incredibly cost effective since you only pay for the service when you use it. Most importantly, OPI allows you to effectively communicate with all of your customers, employees, patients, and communities, thereby making it easier for your organization to successfully carry out its mission.

Jeder Diebstahl von Maßkrügen etc. wird zur Anzeige gebracht!!!
Each theft of mugs etc. is brought to the announcement!!!

A sign in an airport

CHAPTER 21
Video Remote Interpretation

Demand for Video Remote Interpretation (VRI) is growing at an unprecedented rate due to the many advantages it offers compared to over the phone and onsite interpretation. When onsite interpreting services are not immediately available, VRI technology provides a crucial tool in facilitating communication in situations when visual communication with the interpreter is needed.

VRI uses videoconferencing technology that only requires either a cellular connectivity or high-speed Internet connection with sufficient bandwidth or cellular connectivity to reach an interpreter. These interpreters are able to connect to limited English proficient (LEP) or Deaf and Hard of Hearing individuals all over the world in a fraction of the time that it would take an onsite interpreter, but with the visual ability that individuals do not receive from over the phone interpretation.

How VRI Works

Once your VRI service is installed, you can connect on-demand to an interpreter through a simple and easy to use interface. The user simply selects the language, whether they need audio or video, and then the call is connected to the appropriate interpreter.

The best solutions offer an all-in-one option for accessing an interpreter, regardless of whether you need video or audio languages. You can reach a telephone interpreter directly with just the touch of a button by using the VRI device. Not all solutions have the same type of capabilities or connect time, so it is highly recommended when choosing a vendor to have them demonstrate their VRI solution.

From a financial perspective, a key benefit of VRI is that it is more cost effective than hiring an onsite interpreter. VRI is a pay-as-you-go model. Furthermore, unlike onsite interpretation, users do not incur charges for travel or for downtime during an appointment when an interpreter is not needed.

Technological Advancements

It is important to partner with a language access company that continuously evolves alongside the needs of LEP and Deaf and Hard of Hearing individuals. Advancement in VRI technology is paramount in delivering effective language access. New and updated technology results in reduced disruption to services and ensures all video calls are secure. Similar to OPI, technological advancements in the form of a cloud-based platform enable call routing to an interpreter at the fastest connect time possible for all video calls. Business continuity is designed into the cloud-based architecture, and fault tolerance and redundant network design are at the core of the platform to ensure safe and confidential video interpretation sessions. To maintain compliance with privacy regulations, all connections through video calls should be encrypted end to end. The underlying technology should use Web Real-Time Communication (WebRTC) for video calls and secure VoIP for audio calls. With WebRTC, data and video streams should be encrypted using industry standard encryption methods like HTTPS, DTLS, and SRTP.

The language industry has expanded its technological boundaries through the creation of online applications. Apps like LanguageLine's InSight are state-of-the-art technologies that provide a direct, one-click, on-demand connection to interpreters. This industry-leading solution is no longer bound by a Wi-Fi connection, allowing language access from anywhere around the world.

With the ability to use cellular connectivity, the VRI application is designed to deliver total remote access to interpreters, facilitating faster responses to support LEP or Deaf and Hard of Hearing users.

Implementation

As part of the process for setting up video interpreting services, proper vendors will offer implementation services to train your staff on how to use VRI technology. An implementation team will teach your staff to properly utilize video equipment in order to correctly connect LEP, Deaf, and Hard of Hearing individuals to a video interpreter. While you are able to use your own camera-enabled devices, like iPhones, iPads and laptops, some vendors will sell their own devices. Whichever device you choose to use, the implementation process should include training on these devices to ensure your staff is always in compliance.

Implementation training should entail the following:

- How to identify the preferred language of the client to provide the appropriate language support and maintain compliance with regulatory requirements,
- How to work effectively with a professional interpreter to ensure good communication,
- Introduction and training of staff on VRI software and using it on video-enabled device(s),
- In-depth training for Director of Interpreting and related staff, and
- Train the trainer classes for ongoing support.

The Guide to Translation and Localization

For effective implementation, there are certain questions you should ask in order to understand the vendors' process and qualifications. Here are a few questions you should ask a provider:

- Who is your implementation manager and what is her/his experience level?
- Will your IT resources work with ours to establish a secure, encrypted connection?
- Who will be overseeing my implementation?
- Will you provide free training materials?
- Can you train for multiple solutions at the same time, such as telephone interpreting and video remote interpretation?
- Will training take place onsite or remotely?
- What type of support is offered for implementing our video program?

Compliance

Requirements for interpretation assistance were once extremely challenging to meet, but with video remote technology, any organization can be fully compliant with all language access regulations. A secure platform and a proper implementation process are vital to ensure compliance. Among the laws and regulations that video remote interpreting can help your organization comply with are:

- The Americans with Disabilities Act
- Joint Commission Standards
- American Medical Association Code of Medical Ethics, Opinion 9.12
- Title VI of the Civil Rights Act of 1964, Policy on the Prohibition Against National Origin Discrimination as it Affects Persons with Limited English Proficiency
- Executive Order 13166, Improving Access to Services for Persons with Limited English Proficiency
- Health Insurance Portability and accountability Act (HIPAA)

Choosing a VRI Provider

Not all VRI solutions are equal. As with other language services, you get what you pay for, so it is important to approach the vendor selection process just as carefully as you would any other decision that affects your business. As you have read, many factors go into choosing the right vendor for your needs. With that in mind, here are some questions to ask:

- How long have you been offering this service?
- What are the languages that you provide?
- Number of languages available on demand?
- Are your VRI ASL interpreters nationally certified?
- How many seconds does it take to connect to a video interpreter?
- How often do your VRI calls roll over to audio-only interpretation due to lack of video interpreter availability?
- What are your annual average VRI call volumes?
- Please describe any special features of your VRI application?

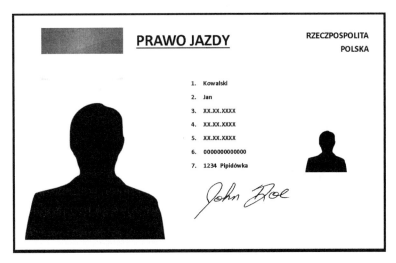

The Irish Police apparently have no in-house translation staff. They have been hunting for one "Prawo Jazdy," a Polish serial offender with over 50 driving violations, who gave a different home address every time he was stopped. The mystery was solved when they discovered that Prawo Jazdy means "driver's license" in Polish.

BBC News, February 19, 2009

The Guide to Translation and Localization

- Is your video solution available on any video enabled device or is certain equipment required? Please include pricing for any required equipment.
- If no specialized equipment is required, what equipment options are available for our video program?
- What are the minimum bandwidth requirements for connecting to a video interpreter through your solution?
- How are video calls encrypted?
- What technical support do you provide for VRI?

As with purchasing other language solutions, you will want to focus on understanding the skill level of interpreters on the video platform. The best American Sign Language (ASL) interpreters are nationally certified through the Registry of Interpreters for the Deaf (RID), but some providers will connect to less expensive and less experienced resources. Similarly, be sure to ask if video interpreters for spoken languages have completed an in-house interpreter training programs and passed language proficiency assessments.

Conclusion

Video remote interpreting provides the visual benefits of onsite interpreting, along with the convenience, speed and cost effectiveness of on-demand access. The ability to see body language and facial expressions as well as to read visual cues reduces the risk of misunderstanding and builds immediate trust, rapport, and cooperation by communicating in-language, person-to-person.

Chapter 22
Onsite Interpretation

Sometimes using an Over-the-Phone Interpreter (OPI) or a Video Remote Interpreter (VRI) is not appropriate, especially in situations that are delicate or serious in nature. In these types of stressful situations, the physical presence of an interpreter can make an individual feel more comfortable and can help the interpreter understand the full scope of a situation.

Onsite interpreting, often referred to as in-person or face-to-face interpreting, is precisely what the words imply. The human interaction and visual contact that onsite interpretation provides can be critical to the success of bridging the communication barrier. In many cases, onsite interpretation may be the only way to communicate effectively with LEPs, Deaf and Hard of Hearing people. This chapter will further explain when and why to use onsite interpretation.

When to Use Onsite Interpretation
Onsite interpretation is the preferred method in situations involving:

- High levels of interaction with multiple participants and unstructured turn-taking
- Complex, critical and sensitive situations
- Intricate dialogue exchanges
- Abstract philosophical interchanges
- Dialogue with veiled intentions or multiple meanings
- Young children or people with under-developed language skills
- High use of idiosyncratic language patterns
- Individuals with a disability that impedes their ability to utilize technology (e.g., poor vision)
- Behavioral and mental health issues

Let us look at some scenarios where the use of onsite interpretation is beneficial for the following industries.

Health Care
Onsite interpreting is often used in high-touch medical settings where verbal cues or sight translations are important in guaranteeing accurate diagnoses and appropriate treatment. Onsite interpreters may act as a conduit for communication during admissions, patient diagnoses, and explanation of treatment plans. This type of situation might involve the patient to move from one room to the next, speaking to multiple people. Onsite interpretation is the ideal solution in assisting the patient and staff to move through the appointment with ease. In-person interpreters are especially appropriate for "end of life" and other sensitive or difficult conversations related to mortality and complex diagnoses where lifespan is uncertain in a medical setting.

In mental health facilities, onsite interpretation might be an effective mode of communication in situations when a patient is unable to differentiate reality from delusions. In this type of scenario, a patient cannot be expected to effectively communicate with an interpreter through a video screen or a phone.

The Guide to Translation and Localization

ASK AN EXPERT:

How will new technologies reshape the role of human translators?

Tex Texin, XenCraft Founder, Chief Architect and Xen Master

Technology is changing not only the execution of translation, but the way in which translators relate to their clients. Today translators are recruited and given assignments via workflow tools. Content can be partitioned, auctioned off, scheduled, distributed to translators, and reintegrated via software. Discussion of the project is entirely via electronic communication. Translators are therefore insulated from their clients and if they are not careful, will not have personalized business relationships with them. It may be possible to do well based purely on the quality of your deliverables. However, it is hard to stand out or to offer value-add services through a software interconnect. Translators may benefit from receiving work via the cloud at salaries and terms dictated by auction, but to have a fulfilling career experience, translators will want strategies to engage clients on a personal level, marketing themselves for unique opportunities and maintaining connections and arranging business outside the cloud job auctions.

Government

It is vital to have onsite interpretation available to not only bridge the language barrier for LEP, Deaf and Hard of Hearing individuals, but also to close the cultural gap by helping these individuals understand laws and regulations.

Onsite services are ideal for encounters between lawyers and clients. This could be for meetings, depositions, hearings, mediations, or any other matter where an attorney needs to communicate with a client in precise detail. The court system also relies on onsite interpreters to support a wide variety of legal proceedings at the local, state and federal level. Some of these settings include:

- Arraignments
- Bail/Bond Reviews
- Preliminary Hearings
- Traffic Offenses
- Fine Payment
- Family Law Centers
- Victim and Witness Interviews
- Public Information
- Clerk Counters
- Juvenile Proceedings

Court qualified interpreters receive specialized training, so they can interpret accurately and follow the correct protocol for legal and courtroom settings.

Business

For those engaged in global trade and business negotiations, the presence of an onsite interpreter is often necessary to finalize a contract or properly communicate in a meeting. Onsite interpretation is the only mode of interpreting that can facilitate situations that involve fluid, nonstop interpretation. This is known as simultaneous interpreting, this type of interpretation is commonly used for large conferences or meetings where there is interaction with multiple speakers and less structured turn taking.

Selecting the Right Language Service Provider

Now that you know some of the scenarios where onsite interpretation is necessary, the next step is to figure out the best vendor to work with the scenarios your company may come across. When shopping for vendors, here are some useful questions for measuring their quality of onsite service:

Reliability and Experience of Provider

- How long have you been offering this service?
- What is your annual revenue?
- What languages do you offer for onsite interpretation?
- What is your fill rate? (This is the percentage of onsite interpretation requests that result in an actual assignment—an important measure.)
- Do you accept requests for assignments at all hours of the day, or are hours limited?
- Do you offer an online portal for requesting interpreters?
- Do you have a team of schedulers?
- If a client requires a certain language that you do not offer, what resources do you have to find interpreters that are able to speak this language?
- How much advanced notice is needed to request an onsite interpreter?
- Do you have a system in place to find interpreters by mileage?

Interpreter Requirements and Qualifications

- How do you screen ASL interpreters?
- Are your ASL interpreters nationally certified?
- How do you screen spoken language interpreters?
- How much experience does a typical interpreter at your organization have?
- Do you have a program for monitoring onsite interpreters? If so, please describe.
- Who conducts pre-hire screening and post-hire monitoring?
- Does your screening process include background checks?
- Do you have a dress code policy?
- Do interpreters sign a code of conduct and code of ethics?
- Do you test or train your interpreters? If so, what is included in these training programs?

ASK AN EXPERT:

Where do you see the language services industry in 5 years?

Salvatore "Salvo" Giammarresi, PayPal Head of Content & Globalization

If the past five years are any indication, I don't expect the language industry to be much different five years later. What I would like to see in that time frame is meaningful innovation that powers more robust and user-friendly tools that are truly designed around the users.

The Guide to Translation and Localization

ASK AN EXPERT:
What does language access mean now to your organization? In 5 years?

Toos Stoker, TAUS
Digital Marketing Director

Machine Translation (MT) has come a long way helping people with their day-to-day simple communications across language barriers. What we hope to see is that in the next 5 years MT is so much improved it can be established as the new lingua franca realizing effective and adequate communication across the languages spoken in the world.

Finding the right language provider that fits with your company's mission is essential. Questions that ask for details about the quality of interpreters, interpreter availability levels, and vendor history not only inform you of the vendor's offerings, but also how they would work as your partner. The value of accuracy and professionalism cannot be underestimated, especially when onsite interpreters are depended on to interpret complex, stressful, and sensitive conversations.

Conclusion

The personal interaction with onsite interpreting is vital in sensitive and complex situations that cannot be properly handled through OPI and VRI. The physical presence of an interpreter can be essential in fulfilling a successful interpretation session. Knowing your LEP, Deaf and Hard of Hearing customers' needs and understanding what modality best fits each of their language access situations is essential to properly bridging language barriers.

A sign in a Chinese train station

CHAPTER 23
Language Proficiency Testing

LanguageLine Academy for Screening and Improved Employee Performance

Screening Bilingual Employees

Some organizations, perhaps yours, hire their own pool of interpreters or bilingual speakers to interact with limited English proficient (LEP) clients. But how do you know that they speak a second language *well* enough to communicate effectively? After all, you probably don't want to hire someone who speaks a "little" Spanish or Mandarin.

Many of us picked up a foreign language in school or while spending time with friends who speak other languages. Determining an employee's proficiency levels in a foreign language and English protects against error and unnecessary harm, improves compliance and protects your company's reputation. What if your LEP client makes a request and the self-identified bilingual employee misunderstands them? Now, it doesn't take a big imagination to understand why screening is so important.

Verification of language proficiency requires the help of experts. Fortunately, there are a few companies, including LanguageLine, that offer testing and training of in-house bilingual resources to verify if they have "native level" and "near native level" proficiency in their declared language.

When selecting a vendor for language assessments, it is important to confirm who created the tests. The assessments offered by LanguageLine Academy, for example, were developed by top academics in the field of translation and test creation.

Trouble shooting:
> If the car do not stay on the drawn track,
draw a thicker line or switch to a different marker or crayon.
Line must be a quarter inch thickness totally filled.

Important:
> Please don't play the inductive truck in
the sun and near a daylight lamp or on the shining paper.

Instructions from an imported toy truck

Applications for Language Proficiency and Interpretation Testing

The need for language testing exists in every industry. Inside the health care field, responsible managers increasingly are seeking out ways to know when their doctors and other medical staff are qualified to either interpret in another language, or speak in a foreign language alone, to LEP patients. Because the job of interpreting for LEPs about medical issues requires a strong knowledge of medical terminology and an excellent foundation in interpreting, you will want to use a proficiency test that measures both vocabulary and interpreting skills. While some LSPs may offer just one general health care test, others can offer a test that verifies the proficiency level for a full-time medical interpreter, another separate test for clinicians who wish to converse with patients in their native language, and a less advanced test for administrative staff working in the health care field.

Private sector businesses, from restaurants to security agencies, also can order language tests. For example, if you own a large restaurant chain and employ managers who know "a little" Spanish or "some" Korean for speaking with LEP workers, maybe their "medium good" language skills are not a big deal at first glance. But what happens when these managers try to deliver health and safety training in their non-native language, and the LEPs who report to them don't understand his directions? Proficiency tests could identify that you would be better off hiring face-to-face interpreters or even using a video-remote or over the phone interpreter for these sessions to ensure that your employees understand these important sessions.

As you might expect, the cost, type, and effectiveness of language assessment tests vary from one vendor to the next. And, like most services, if you purchase based on price alone, the feedback you receive about your employees' language proficiency skills may not be what you are seeking. To give you an idea of the kinds of tests that are available in the marketplace, here are some of the ones LanguageLine offers:

Language Proficiency Test (LPT)

The LPT is designed in the format of an oral proficiency interview in one language that follows the candidate's interests and strengths within a general conversational context. Examiners are trained to take the candidate through progressively more challenging linguistic tasks to determine the level at which the candidate can speak the tested language.

Bilingual Fluency Assessment (BFA)

The BFA assesses the candidate's oral proficiency in English and a target language, as well as knowledge of general terminology commonly used in a health care setting by medical assistants, receptionists, and other front end staff.

Bilingual Fluency Assessment for Clinicians (BFAC)

The BFAC assesses the same knowledge as the BFA; however, it includes specific medical terminology in both tested languages. It is often used to assess the fluency of clinical staff in a health care setting, such as physicians, nurses, technicians, etc.

Interpreter Skills Test (IST)

The IST evaluates fluency in English and the tested language, knowledge of basic medical terminology, accuracy of interpreting, attentive listening, information retention, ability to follow instructions, role of the interpreter, presentation and delivery, and customer service skills.

Once the test taker finishes the assessment, expert raters offer detailed feedback and a numerical score for the proficiency level. Not all LSPs offer testing services, and the level of detailed feedback provided by those that do vary significantly.

A Word of Caution

Whether your organization is based in a major metropolitan area where a hundred or more languages are spoken, or a rural area where only a few are, it is often not possible to hire bilingual employees to cover all the languages that may be requested. Fortunately, language service providers offer many options to help you communicate. But if you choose to go it alone, you will need to ask yourself whether you are certain that the people you employ have the requisite skills to do so effectively. Language proficiency testing is the best way to make sure that they do.

Chapter 24

Straight to the Source

How Good Is Your Source Material?

By Charlene Haykel - Director, LanguageLine Clarity^{SM}

We have described how to select a translation vendor. We have also explained when to use video interpretation verus onsite interpretation services. Until now, though, we have seldom had much to say about the source material that begins your journey through the translation and localization process.

Poor ingredients spoil the best recipe. So the quality of your source material matters a lot to the ultimate success of your translation project.

A Clear-Eyed Look At Source Documents

In this chapter, we're going straight to the source—asking you to take a hard look, *before translation*, at how effectively your source material communicates with your intended audiences. With your documents spread out before you, and with as much clear-eyed objectivity as you can muster, ask yourself these questions:

- Is the content of my documents too voluminous, too thin or "just right" for conveying the most critical parts of my organization's message?
- Is there a lot of repetition in the text or a great deal of irrelevant and distracting detail that does not advance the narrative or add value to the reader?
- Are my documents organized logically, with information sections or categories clearly labeled; do subheads and call outs help guide readers through the text?
- Are the documents visually daunting, chock full of print (and fine print) top to bottom and side to side? Are they something I, myself, might toss at first glance?
- And finally, are my documents likely to be understood by someone who is not an expert in my field?

Is My Source Material "Too Much"?

The truth is that most printed material flowing through businesses and government agencies has 20-30% more copy than it needs to communicate core content clearly and effectively to end users. Not only does this excess, noncore content not advance your message, it actually obstructs it—and at a high cost to you and your organization. You lose your audience in a fog of confusion, you lose their good will and loyalty to your brand, and sometimes, you even lose their trust. And you pay dearly to print, update and, yes, *translate*, all those extra burdensome words.

As a language service provider, LanguageLine has no choice but to translate—and charge for—every incomprehensible and unnecessary word our clients submit with their source materials. As a result, what we ultimately deliver to our clients, while expertly translated, will not always fulfill the promise of providing easy access across languages and cultures.

Simplifying Source Material

There is a little-known subspecialty within the marketing communications field that can help resolve the conundrum of flawed source material. Simplified communications, as it is called, improves the quality of all the "ingredients" that go into your communications "stew." Its techniques and processes take a sharp pencil to source text, searching for and eliminating unnecessary, noncore content.

Conversely, its analytic techniques also help to surface content that is essential to the concerns of both author and audience. This core content becomes the connective material that, when translated, will effectively link people and ideas across countries and cultures.

By streamlining documents before translation, simplification techniques create clear, comprehensible source material that will become clear comprehensible documents in every other language into which they're translated.

Simplified Communications is offered by a small number of freelance practitioners or small boutique practices around the country. Never before, however, has it been offered by a language services company.

Because LanguageLine believes that the clarity and effectiveness of source material has a direct impact on the quality of the related translations, we recently introduced a new solution called LanguageLine Clarity^{SM}.

Languageline Clarity^{SM}

LanguageLine Clarity^{SM} effectively adds a new language—i.e., plain English— to our translation portfolio. It also provides our clients with a powerful, trademarked tool for simplifying entire communication programs or categories. Typical examples include forms, brochures, and fact sheets. With LanguageLine Clarity^{SM}, we can seamlessly convert flawed source material into effective, communicative documents in 240 languages.

Through Clarity^{SM}, we offer two kinds of simplified communications:

Microsimplification is the plain English translation and redesign of individual documents, without reference to any other communications.

Macrosimplification® is our proprietary process that applies simplification principles and tactics to entire communication systems within an organization. It is designed to achieve content consolidation across product, division and service lines and to create more efficient and cost-effective communications for all audiences.

Charlene Haykel

I'm paid to write clear, spare prose — I talk nonstop for free. Writing or talking, language has always been my thing. Majored in English; studied Latin and French; and these days, every Tuesday night, I wrestle Italian to the ground. Love every minute of it. In the interest of showing off ... my sentiments, in Italian, about joining LanguageLine:

Adesso, voglio dire che sia tanto felice essere qui, a LanguageLine. Ed, anticipo il piacere di lavorare con miei colleghi ed cliente per fare i mezzi chiari ed comprehensible comunicazione a tutti.

Clients can benefit from both these simplification services in the following ways:

From Microsimplification:

- Organizations will ensure that their translated content is comprehensible to end-users of any country or culture and any literacy or education level;
- Clients in government and regulated industries can achieve compliance with language access regulations during the translation process, saving time and money;
- All clients will substantially improve the the return on their investment in translation and localization through the substantial word- and page-count reductions typically achieved with simplification.

From Macrosimplification®:

- Clients will right-size their communication systems across the enterprise;
- Clients will substantially reduce their marketing and corporate communication costs, by 20-30% and more;
- Clients will improve customers' and stakeholders' experiences through fewer, simpler and clearer communications;
- Clients will begin to imbed a culture of simplification within their own organizations. With simplification training services from LanguageLine Solutions, they will acquire the knowledge and skill-sets needed to create better source materials in-house.

By translating them into plain English before they are converted to another language, and improving their content, structure and design, all documents can benefit from LanguageLine Clarity^{SM}. Here are the primary benefits:

- Your documents will be crystal clear to all your audiences, no matter what language they speak.
- They will also be far less costly to translate, produce, distribute and maintain.
- Finally, your documents will help your organization become both an effective and cost-effective communicator across the globe.

Results like these translate well into any language.

CHAPTER 25
Builders, Breakers and Defenders

An article that is not about translation technology ...

By Vanessa Eke - Managing Director, LanguageLine UK

If I had a dollar, a pound, or even a rupee for every article on translation security that I've seen circulating over the last 3 years, I'd be rich.

Security is one of the largest growth industries in the world and surprise, surprise, has become the latest obsession of everyone from Trump Tower to Tinseltown.

Cybersecurity insurance is one of the fastest growing sectors in the insurance market, according to the PwC Global State of Information Security Survey 2016. A recent PwC report forecasts that the global cyber insurance market will reach $7.5 billion in annual sales by 2020, up from $2.5 billion this year.

It is said by some that the combined revenue from security products and services has probably out-run the "actual" damage caused by security breaches many times over. Believe me, this article won't change that one iota as global paranoia reaches an all-time high. It's arguably the best market in the world to be playing in.

The translation industry is therefore now racing along with all the other corporate content providers to prove that it is leading in the field of safety, security and privacy, and therefore offering the very best solutions to the market.

Our customers already know about firewalls, data encryption and phishing. They know not to send classified emails from public Wi-Fi hotspots or have their laptop open with sensitive data on the train. We don't need to repeat the same message until the page turns yellow.

I would rather turn the topic on its head and say that translation security is about three things: Enforcing Discipline, Making Good Choices, and Managing Risk.

I have an admission to make. As an individual I use Google Translate all the time. If I want a quick and dirty view of a publicly available document knowing that I only need the gist of the content? Bang—cut and paste and in it goes. Job done. Doesn't everyone? Who cares if Google sees it, owns it, or regurgitates it. It wasn't mine in the first place and it doesn't matter.

If, however, I need to produce something for customer consumption, such as integrated marketing campaigns, websites, legal documents, or manuals, then I may as well get it right first time and on-time, at the best price I can buy for the appropriate quality I'm looking for. Some of this may need to be secure, some of it may need to be secret, and some of it may require multiple step security protocols.

Assuming that you only use ISO 27001 certified suppliers, like LanguageLine, then you've already reduced the risk dramatically. It's a damned hard certification to both qualify for and keep hold of in this industry. That takes care of secure process assurance and secure third party supplier management. The homework has already been done for you.

The Guide to Translation and Localization

In China, Microsoft's search engine Bing sounds like "illness" or "pancake" when spoken in local dialects, depending on the tone. Microsoft executives there then made the search engine's Chinese name biying, which also referred to a longer Chinese expression you qui bi ying, which roughly means "seek and ye shall find."

For the most part, in the regular world of translation of standard documents, this is as far as you can or would want to secure the data: Secure systems; NDAs; and well-briefed, professionally-qualified translators, proofreaders and project managers who are monitored and measured are as much as you need. For more sensitive work you could throw in some rotation and additional encryption and you're done.

At the client side, we suggest you make security as easy as possible. Linking into a secure project management system that is user friendly means no uploading and downloading of data, and less chance of a slip-up or staff trying to short-circuit complex, over-worked or lengthy processes.

If documents are super-sensitive then give certain words code-names. (Just don't forget to decode before the final is released inside your own systems which should ideally be secured to ISO 27001 standards.)

If security protocols are an integrated part of working practice, then far less enforcement is required. It becomes the way the job is done, and just happens to be the most secure way of working ... and hey—presto—it's also the easiest and most transparent way of managing projects.

I haven't written this article in a light-hearted fashion to make light of security, which is a serious subject. I wrote it to illustrate that the more it becomes an obsession in its own right then the less likely it is to be integrated within normal business process and the more likely it is to fail.

Choose a language services provider with an emphasis on the safety and security of your data from start to finish as part of the quality of the service, with an end-to-end view of how it keeps the data secure, with policies and practices that reinforce this with its staff and suppliers, and with teeth when these policies are not adhered to.

Documents are best marked with security levels (say, 1-5) using your company's own view of what that means. The translation company can then be briefed on this and help you take appropriate steps depending on the level required. If you need "white room" level security where translators are searched upon entering and leaving a secure room and are experts in a specific field of say, LIBOR, then expect to pay a premium. If you are translating a retail catalogue for the 50th time with minor changes, then a healthy dose of TM with proofreading of new entries should just about do it at a much lower cost.

One final thought. Security is all about managing risk. Most organizations have so much confidential information visible around the office that it gives the game away. I would say the risk is far less about the translated material than the everyday office environment and what is left on white boards, documents by printers, chats on the subway and in the pub.

If you would like a serious conversation about what we have to offer, and I mean offer what you "really" need within the realms of the timelines, budgets and protocols that work for you then please do email me personally at Vanessa.eke@languageline.co.uk and I promise you won't be disappointed. Over here we do everything back to front as well as front to back. The whole process starts with you, not us, and you can reach me from 8 am to 6 pm which means we can talk whether you are in Munich, Manchester or Melbourne.

No entry for heavy goods vehicles. Residential site only

←

Nid wyf yn y swyddfa ar hyn o bryd. Anfonwch unrhyw waith i'w gyfieithu.

A sign in Wales. Translation: "I am not in the office at the moment. Send any work to be translated."

Contact Information - Contributors

LanguageLine Solutions	**LanguageLine Translation Solutions** 15115 SW Sequoia Parkway Suite 100 Portland, OR 97224 Ph: 1-503-419-4856 • Fax: 1-503-419-4873 Toll Free: 800-878-8523 Email: info@LLTS.com www.LLTS.com	
LanguageLine Solutions	**LanguageLine - U.K. Headquarters** 25th Floor, 40 Bank Street Canary Wharf London E14 5NR Phone: 0800 169 2879 Email: enquiries@languageline.co.uk www.languageline.com/uk	Chapter 25
LanguageLine Solutions	**LanguageLine Services** 1 Lower Ragsdale Drive, Building 2 Monterey, CA 93940 Toll Free: 1-800-752-6096 option 2 Email: info@languageline.com www.languageline.com	Chapters 20-24
SMARTLING	**Smartling** US HQ 1 (866) 707-6278 hi@smartling.com 1375 Broadway 14th Floor New York, NY 10018 smartling.com London +44 203 880 7958 hi@smartling.com 16 Upper Woburn Place WC1H 0AF, UK Dublin 1 (866) 707-6278 hi@smartling.com 9 Pembroke St. Upper Dublin 2, Ireland	Chapter 17

Laura Brandon, Executive Director

GALA - The Globalization and Localization Association (GALA) is a global, non-profit trade association for the translation and localization industry. As a membership organization, we support our member companies and the corporate language sector by creating communities, championing standards, sharing knowledge, and advancing technology. To learn more about the value of membership, visit www.gala-global.org or follow us @GALA_global.

Florian Faes, Co-Founder of Slator

Slator - Slator makes business sense of the language services and technology market with news on the people and deals that shape the industry. Our platforms include the Slator.com website and bespoke events created to foster high-impact discussions with the industry's decision-makers. Headquartered in Zurich, Switzerland, Slator also has a presence in Singapore and Manila, the Philippines.

Salvatore "Salvo" Giammarresi, Head of Content & Globalization

At PayPal (Nasdaq:PYPL), we put people at the center of everything we do. Founded in 1998, we continue to be at the forefront of the digital payments revolution. PayPal gives people better ways to manage and move their money, offering them choice and flexibility in how they are able to send money, pay or get paid. We operate an open, secure and technology agnostic payments platform that businesses use to securely transact with their customers online, in stores and increasingly on mobile devices.

In 2015, 28% of the 4.9 billion payments we processed were made on a mobile device. With our 192 million active customer accounts, PayPal is a truly global payments platform that is available to people in more than 200 markets, allowing customers to get paid in more than 100 currencies, withdraw funds to their bank accounts in 56 currencies and hold balances in their PayPal accounts in 25 currencies.

Contributors

Winnie Heh, Career & Academic Advisor

MIIS - The Middlebury Institute of International Studies at Monterey offers its students a wide range of professional degrees to prepare them for careers in fields including international business, development, education, environmental policy, language teaching, and translation and interpretation. The Institute's 750 students come from more than 50 countries around the world and together with the faculty share a deep interest in, and commitment to, global engagement and cross-cultural communication. Since it was founded in 1955, the Institute has developed leading programs in these diverse fields of study. Today it is home to research centers and initiatives, including the renowned James Martin Center for Nonproliferation Studies, the Center for the Blue Economy, and others.

Toos Stoker, Digital Marketing Director

TAUS - TAUS is a resource center for the global language and translation industries. Our mission is to increase the size and significance of the translation industry to help the world communicate better.

We envision translation as a standard feature, a utility, similar to the internet, electricity, and water. Translation available in all languages to all people in the world will push the evolution of human civilization to a much higher level of understanding, education, and discovery.

We support buyers and providers of language services and technologies with a comprehensive suite of online services, software, and knowledge that help them to grow and innovate their business. We extend the reach and growth of the translation industry through our vision of the Human Language Project and our execution with sharing translation memory data and quality evaluation metrics.

For more information about TAUS, please visit: https://www.taus.net

Dr. Nitish Singh (Ph.D. MBA, MA), Program Leader

"Global Digital Marketing & Localization Certification" is one of the world's unique educational offerings which combines digital marketing with localization skills for gaining local and global competitive advantage. http://goo.gl/EaoZ9G

The program leads to dual credentials with certificate by University of North Carolina (Wilmington) and industry certification by the Localization Institute.

Learn More: www.certificateindigitalmarketing.com

Tex Texin, Founder, Chief Architect and Xen Master

Xen Craft - XenCraft is a consulting firm specializing in software globalization. XenCraft enhances software and Web applications so that they can be used in markets anywhere in the world. We are experts in Unicode, double-byte encodings, character set conversion, algorithms for efficient text processing, right-to-left language design, and providing support for all locales. XenCraft globalization assessments include analysis of gaps in software internationalization and instructions for correcting the gaps and internationalization testing, localization process improvement and automation. We can provide guidance on machine translation and crowd sourcing and global business and product strategies. We have helped companies in eCommerce, health care, storage, social network, and other industries go global.

Jack Welde, Co-Founder & CEO

Smartling - Smartling's enterprise translation management platform helps brands gain a more competitive global position by transforming the way their content is created and consumed around the world. Smartling's technology helps brands access new markets, more customers, and greater value. The company is headquartered in NYC with more than 150 employees spread across its 5 global offices. For more information, please visit www.smartling.com.

For our clients, language access is within a finger's reach.

LanguageLine enables your customers, constituents, and patients to easily communicate with anyone in your organization using one of our Language ID Cards.

Use this card to identify which language they need, and one of our expert interpreters will be on the line, on your screen, or in your office in no time to help.

LanguageLine Solutions' Interpreters are available in more than 240 languages and American Sign Language, 24 hours a day, seven days a week to communicate with limited English proficient or Deaf or Hard-of-Hearing individuals.

- Present this guide to determine which language to request.
- Languages are listed alphabetically.
- The individual only needs to point to their preferred language.

Visit www.LanguageLine.com or call 1-800-752-6096 for more information on all our language access solutions:

- Phone, video, and onsite interpreting
- Translation and Localization
- Bilingual staff and interpreter testing and training

CustomerCare@LanguageLine.com

1-800-752-6096

# Language Identification Card

English Translation: Point to your language. An interpreter will be called. The interpreter is provided at no cost to you.

Arabic — عربي ☞	**Korean** — 한국어 ☞
أشر إلى لغتك. وسيتم الاتصال بمترجم فوري. كما سيتم إحضار المترجم الفوري مجانًا.	귀하께서 사용하는 언어를 지정하시면 해당 언어 통역 서비스를 무료로 제공해 드립니다.
Burmese — မြန်မာ ☞	**Mandarin** — 國語 ☞
သင့်ဘာသာစကားကို ညွှန်ပြပါ။ စကားပြန် ခေါ်ပေးပါမယ်။ သင့်အတွက် စကားပြန် အခမဲ့ ပေးပါမယ်။	请指认您的语言，以便为您提供免费的口译服务。
Cantonese — 廣東話 ☞	**Polish** — Polski ☞
請指認您的語言，以便為您提供免費的口譯服務。	Proszę wskazać swój język i wezwiemy tłumacza. Usługa ta zapewniana jest bezpłatnie.
Farsi — فارسی ☞	**Portuguese** — Português ☞
زبان مورد نظر خود را مشخص کنید. یک مترجم برای شما درخواست خواهد شد. مترجم بصورت رایگان در اختیار شما قرار می گیرد.	Indique o seu idioma. Um intérprete será chamado. A interpretação é fornecida sem qualquer custo para você.
French — Français ☞	**Punjabi** — ਪੰਜਾਬੀ ☞
Indiquez votre langue et nous appellerons un interprète. Le service est gratuit.	ਆਪਣੀ ਭਾਸ਼ਾ ਵੱਲ ਇਸ਼ਾਰਾ ਕਰੋ। ਜਿਸ ਮੁਤਾਬਕ ਇੱਕ ਦੁਭਾਸ਼ੀਆ ਬੁਲਾਇਆ ਜਾਵੇਗਾ। ਤੁਹਾਡੇ ਲਈ ਦੁਭਾਸ਼ੀਆ ਦਾ ਮੁਫਤ ਇੰਤਜ਼ਾਮ ਕੀਤਾ ਜਾਂਦਾ ਹੈ।
Haitian Creole — Kreyòl ☞	**Russian** — Русский ☞
Lonje dwèt ou sou lang ou pale a epi n ap rele yon entèprèt pou ou. Nou ba ou sèvis entèprèt la gratis.	Укажите язык, на котором вы говорите. Вам вызовут переводчика. Услуги переводчика предоставляются бесплатно.
Hindi — हिंदी ☞	**Somali** — Af-Soomaali ☞
अपनी भाषा को इंगित करें। जिसके अनुसार आपके लिए दुभाषिया बुलाया जाएगा। आपके लिए दुभाषिया की निशुल्क व्यवस्था की जाती है।	Farta ku fiiqluqadaada… Waxa laguugu yeeri doonaa turjubaan. Turjubaanka wax lacagi kaaga bixi mayso.
Hmong — Hmoob ☞	**Spanish** — Español ☞
Taw rau koj hom lus. Yuav hu rau ib tug neeg txhais lus. Yuav muaj neeg txhais lus yam uas koj tsis tau them dab tsi.	Señale su idioma y llamaremos a un intérprete. El servicio es gratuito.
Italian — Italiano ☞	**Tagalog** — Tagalog ☞
Indicare la propia lingua. Un interprete sarà chiamato. Il servizio è gratuito.	Ituro po ang inyong wika. Isang tagasalin ang ipagkakaloob nang libre sa inyo.
Japanese — 日本語 ☞	**Vietnamese** — Tiếng Việt ☞
あなたの話す言語を指してください。無料で通訳サービスを提供します。	Hãy chỉ vào ngôn ngữ của quý vị. Một thông dịch viên sẽ được gọi đến, quý vị sẽ không phải trả tiền cho thông dịch viên.

Language Solutions: Over-the-Phone, Video Remote, and Onsite Interpreting / Bilingual and Interpreter Staff Testing and Training / Translation and Localization

www.LanguageLine.com

© 2018 LanguageLine Solutions

LanguageLine® InSight Video Interpreting℠
Reliable • Easy • Secure • Robust

LanguageLine InSight video remote interpreting (VRI) empowers you to provide outstanding service and exceptional care, on-demand, to the Limited English Proficient and the Deaf and Hard-of-Hearing through The Power of Sight℠.

One-touch access to trained professional video interpreters on your PC, tablet or smartphone facilitates full understanding through spoken and visual communication to reduce the risk of misunderstanding by capturing body language and facial expressions to read visual cues.

Our clients rave about InSight:

"We just obtained InSight for use in our emergency room. What a fabulous piece of technology!"
"The system worked beautifully. The sign language translation was very cool."
"First time using—very easy and the interpreter was so professional."

Why Use LanguageLine InSight®?

Having one-touch access to trained professional interpreters enhances productivity, improves service and increases revenue while complying with laws and regulations.

Award-winning LanguageLine InSight Video Interpreting is the fastest, easiest to use, most reliable and secure, video and audio interpreting solution of its kind.

Here are just a few advantages of LanguageLine Insight:
- Video offered in the top 35 languages covering 98% of demand
- Includes American Sign Language
- Audio-only interpreting available 24/7 in more than 240 languages
- On-demand access to nearly 9,000 professional linguists
- Qualified, tested and monitored interpreters with industry-specific training
- Nationally certified American Sign Language interpreters
- High quality video and audio complies with ACA Section 1557
- HIPAA compliant, secure, end-to-end encrypted video and audio
- 24/7 direct LanguageLine technical support
- MDM compatible
- Ability to rate each call after completion
- Available as an iPhone app

Download LanguageLine InSight, our easy to use video interpretation app to access an interpeter anywhere, anytime on your smart device.

InSight is available for iPad and iPhone in the App Store

For Android or Windows PC with Chrome or Firefox browser, use the following link:

https://insight.languageline.com

Phone Interpreting Languages

Some languages may not be available at the time of your call. Not all languages are available in all regions. Additional languages and dialects may be available. Rare languages may require additional interpreter connect time or may require an appointment. If you have a question regarding language availability, please contact your Account Executive or Customer Care.

Acholi	Duala	Jamaican Patois	Mbay	Sicilian
Afar	Dutch	Japanese	Mien	Sinhala
Afrikaans	Dzongkha	Jarai	Mirpuri	Slovak
Akan	Edo	Javanese	Mixteco	Slovene
Akateko	Ekegusii	Jingpho	Mizo	Soga
Albanian	Estonian	Jinyu	Mnong	Somali
Amharic	Ewe	Juba Arabic	Mongolian	Soninke
Anuak	Farsi	Jula	Moroccan Arabic	Sorani
Apache	Fijian	Kaba	Mortlockese	Spanish
Arabic	Fijian Hindi	Kamba	Napoletano	Sudanese Arabic
Armenian	Finnish	Kanjobal	Navajo	Sunda
Assyrian	Flemish	Kannada	Nepali	Susu
Azerbaijani	French	Karen	Ngambay	Swahili
Bahasa	French Canadian	Kashmiri	Nigerian Pidgin	Swedish
Bahdini	Fukienese	Kayah	Norwegian	Sylhetti
Bahnar	Fulani	Kazakh	Nuer	Tagalog
Bajuni	Fuzhou	Kham	Nupe	Taiwanese
Bambara	Ga	Khana	Nyanja	Tajik
Bantu	Gaddang	Khmer	Nyoro	Tamil
Barese	Gaelic-Irish	K'iché	Ojibway	Telugu
Basque	Gaelic-Scottish	Kikuyu	Oromo	Thai
Bassa	Garre	Kimiiru	Pampangan	Tibetan
Belorussian	Gen	Koho	Papiamento	Tigré
Bemba	Georgian	Korean	Pashto	Tigrigna
Benaadir	German	Krahn	Plautdietsch	Toishanese
Bengali	German Penn. Dutch	Krio	Pohnpeian	Tongan
Berber	Gheg	Kunama	Polish	Tooro
Bosnian	Gokana	Kurmanji	Portuguese	Trique
Bravanese	Greek	Kyrgyz	Portuguese Brazilian	Turkish
Bulgarian	Gujarati		Portuguese Cape Verdean	Turkmen
Burmese	Gulay	Laotian	Pugliese	Tzotzil
Cantonese	Gurani	Latvian	Pulaar	Ukrainian
Catalan	Haitian Creole	Liberian Pidgin English	Punjabi	Urdu
Cebuano	Hakka China	Lingala	Putian	Uyghur
Chaldean	Hakka Taiwan	Lithuanian	Quechua	Uzbek
Chamorro	Hassaniyya	Luba-Kasai	Quichua	Vietnamese
Chaochow	Hausa	Luganda	Rade	Visayan
Chin Falam	HawaiianHebrew	Luo	Rakhine	Welsh
Chin Hakha	Hiligaynon	Maay	Rohingya	Wodaabe
Chin Mara	Hindi	Macedonian	Romanian	Wolof
Chin Matu	Hindko	Malay	Rundi	Wuzhou
Chin Senthang	Hmong	Malayalam	Russian	Yemeni Arabic
Chin Tedim	Hunanese	Maltese	Rwanda	Yiddish
Chipewyan	Hungarian	Mam	Samoan	Yoruba
Chuukese	Icelandic	Mandarin	Sango	Yunnanese
Cree	Igbo	Mandinka	Seraiki	Zapoteco
Croatian	Ilocano	Maninka	Serbian	Zarma
Czech	Indonesian	Manobo	Shanghainese	Zo
Danish	Inuktitut	Marathi	Shona	Zyphe
Dari	Italian	Marka	Sichuan Yi	
Dewoin	Jakartanese	Marshallese		
Dinka		Masalit		